Life In T

THE WEST

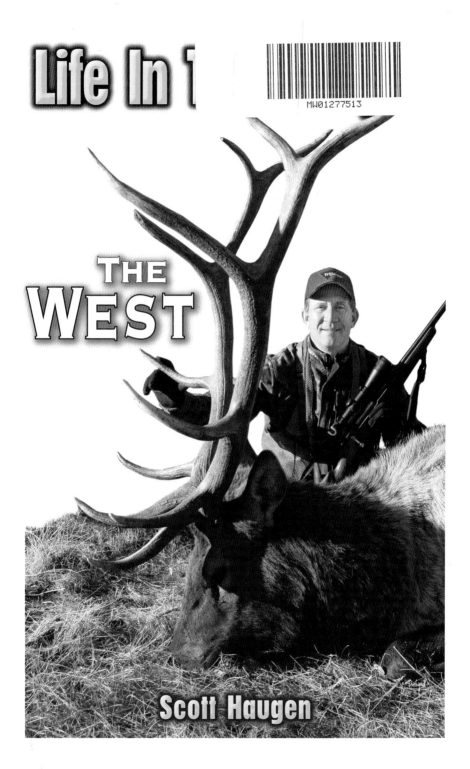

Scott Haugen

MW01277513

H E

Dedication

This book is dedicated to each and
every hunter who aspires to
live the dream.

© Scott Haugen

All rights reserved. No part of this publication may be used or repro-
duced in any from without permission from the author.

Published by:
Haugen Enterprises
2009, Springfield, OR

Softbound ISBN-13: 978-0-9819423-1-5

All photographs taken by the author unless otherwise noted.
www.scotthaugen.com

Book and cover design by Tony Amato

Printed in Singapore

1 3 5 7 9 10 8 6 4 2

Contents

Acknowledgments

Without the help and support of people, I would not be living the life I am today. Thanks to all the friends, guides, outfitters, publishers, editors and television producers I've worked with over the years. Without you, this book would not have been possible.

I'd like to extend a special thanks to some key people who created opportunities for me, who believed in and supported me in all my endeavors. To Craig Boddington and Jim Zumbo, whose support in the writing world got me started in the outdoor industry. To the folks at Wolf Creek Productions, Media Jungle, the Outdoor Channel and Trijicon, without you my television shows would not have been possible.

Especially, I'd like to thank my parents, Jerry and Jean Haugen, and my beloved wife and children, Tiffany, Braxton and Kazden Haugen, for your constant support, encouragement and unconditional love. You are the real reason I'm able to live the dream and share my experiences with the rest of God's great world.

Introduction

Prior to entering into the outdoor industry, full-time, I was a science teacher for 12 years. In fact, both my wife, Tiffany, and I were school teachers. We started teaching in Oregon, then spent much of the 1990s in two very remote Inupiat Eskimo villages on Alaska's desolate North Slope. From there, we taught at an international school in Sumatra, Indonesia.

The year 2000 marked a time of major change in my life. Not only did my first son enter the world, but my first book, *Hunting The Alaskan High Arctic*, was published. I'd written for several hunting and fishing magazines in multiple countries by that time and truly loved the experience. When Tiffany and I moved back home to where we both grew up in Walterville, Oregon, east of Eugene, I ran the idea by her of my taking a year off teaching.

By the amount of work I was getting from magazines, I was confident I'd be able to eek out a living from hunting and fishing. When Tiffany smiled and encouraged me to go for it, I about cried. From that moment, I knew my life would not be the same.

Since then, I haven't been back to the classroom. Perhaps one day I will, as I never know what lies in the future, but for now, I have what I consider to be the best job in the world. Since Tiffany's words of encouragement, I've been blessed to have more than 1,000 magazine articles published around the globe in some of the world's most prestigious outdoor magazines. I've hosted a handful of television shows, filming more than 250 episodes to date. I've also fulfilled my desires of educating and talking to others through conducting more than 40 seminars a year.

Of all the hats I wear in this business, writing is what I'm most passionate about. Sitting down at my computer is when I can crawl into my little shell, shut myself off from the rest of the world and relive cherished moments in the field.

I grew up in a hunting oriented family, and have been shooting guns since I could walk. Combining the knowledge I've picked up through hunting around the world, and what I learned through my formal education – I majored in geography, with a minor in biology and earned a Masters Degree in education from the University of Oregon – I've put myself in the very unique situation of being able to hunt for a living. For this I am blessed and very thankful. Every morning I wake up and every night I go to bed, I thank God for allowing me to live this life, for He's the one who has continually prepared me for the next journey, whatever it may be. I couldn't imagine doing anything else that I love more, not at this stage in my life.

Normally, in this line of work, I spend more than 250 days in the field each year. What I learn during these times is information I want to share with others. One of my biggest motivators is to share information with fellow hunters so they can find success in their future hunting adventures. I do this through television, speaking, writing magazine articles and penning books.

Of all the writing I do, the style that lies closest to my heart is reliving the hunt. These adventure stories take me back to the moment, allowing me to bring to life the sights, smells, ups and downs and the thrills of every experience. That's the purpose of this book, to share the blessings I've experienced, and better yet, make you a part of it.

While I've been fortunate to hunt around the world, my heart lies in the American West. This is where I grew up, and this is where I love to hunt. Don't get me wrong, I won't pass up an opportunity to hunt Africa, New Zealand, South America, or any other corner of the globe. I love those places, too. In fact, I love all hunting, no matter what the species or tool I'm hunting with.

Personally, hunting is what takes me to other places in the world, destinations I would not otherwise see. It allows me to meet people, learn more about the land and its history, observe cultures and gain a deeper understanding and appreciation of traditions. I'm not the kind of person to climb a 10,000-foot mountain to see the view or to watch a sunset, but if there's a sheep to hunt at the top, I'm there.

Following is a collection of stories capturing some of my most memorable big game hunts in the American West, and what made them so special. It is my fondest wish that you enjoy reading them as much as I did living and reliving them.

Live The Dream,

—Scott Haugen

Foreword

As a person who has been writing articles about hunting for more than 45 years, I'm naturally drawn to the "new" scribes of the day. I often look at their bylines, read their work, and make a judgement call as to their credibility and chances of making it in the business. There's an old saying in the industry: "There are hunters who write, and writers who hunt." Indeed, many outdoor journalists are wordsmiths but are woefully inept in the outdoors. Their articles may be gripping, but now and then I have to ask myself if I'm reading fact or fiction.

Not so with Scott Haugen. My take on Scott is crystal clear. He is both a hunter who writes and a writer who hunts. He lives the life; he's the real deal. Scott is a tough, savvy outdoorsman, who punches his tag more often than not and usually leaves the woods with meat in his pack. Many of those hunts are unguided, where Scott embraces the wilderness on his own terms and wins the game of successfully challenging his quarry.

I'm intrigued with Scott's background. He and his lovely wife, Tiffany, taught school in two Inupiat communities on Alaska's north slope, living under the harshest conditions in all of North America. Another teaching stint in Indonesia offered them even more incredible challenges. During those periods, Scott took advantage of the hunting opportunities available, and added to his ever growing collection of memories steeped in adventure.

On occasion, my peers and I reflect on the "new" names in the outdoors, and who, like foam in a chilled beer glass, will rise to the top. No question in my mind, Scott is highest on my list with no close second. I'm continually impressed by his newest achievements, and I don't miss reading any of his stories.

This book chronicles his hunts in North America...so far, and I'm sure there will be many more hunts, and more books. This one will sit on my night stand, and I'm already looking forward to the next.

—Jim Zumbo,
former hunting editor
Outdoor Life magazine

Chapter 1:

King Of The Mountain

Up to this point in my life, the toughest hunts I'd ever been on were for Himalayan tahr and Dall sheep. All of that changed on my quest for a mountain goat.

During my years of living in Alaska, I never had the chance to pursue the white ghosts of the highest pinnacles. The time I spent in Alaska's arctic was miles from mountain goats country, and simply getting to them was too much of a time consuming effort from the little Inupiat Eskimo villages I called home.

I'd hunted Dall sheep in parts of Alaska, and taken some nice rams where I lived in the Brooks Range, but the mountain goat was an animal that eluded me. Finally, after settling back in Oregon, the timing was right.

I met Larry and Lori Warren, owners of renowned Tuchodi River Outfitters, at a Safari Club International convention in Reno. It was January 2008, and in October of that year I found myself in their hunting camp.

Following a short bush plane flight from Fort Nelson, British Columbia, we soon landed in the main camp. Upon our descent through the rugged mountains, goats could be seen grazing high on the granite peaks. The lower our plane got, the higher the surrounding country grew. I was glad I'd been working out – lifting weights, running, mountain biking and hauling heavy loads in my backpack – for the past eight months.

Our mountain goat adventure began with a five hour horseback ride to where we pitched spike camp along the timbered, northeastern shores of Tuchodi Lake. With camp roughed out, we left the wrangler to finish up the final details. From there, Travis Ralls, my ace camera man, Richard Baumeister, our guide, and myself, rode the horses another hour. Breaking into the open, graveled shores along the lake, we found the spot where we'd spend the rest of the day looking for goats.

From here we glassed the vertical, slate-covered cliffs that engulfed us, but we failed to see a goat. Then we broke out the spotting scopes – that's when I learned that this country was even bigger than I imagined.

What land we'd just been looking at through binoculars, revealed goats hidden everywhere. A reality check found me asking if I could even physically make it up to where they were.

"Don't worry, those goats are only a last resort," assured Richard, one of Tuchodi's veteran goat guides. Those were the most encouraging words I'd heard so far.

We glassed right up until dark, and three more goats revealed themselves. From where we watched, along the tranquil shores of the lake, the stalks looked pretty straight forward. Little did I know that by this time the following day, I'd be in the middle of the toughest hunt of my life.

Riding the horses back to spike camp in the dark, the going was peaceful and quiet, save for bugling elk in the surrounding timber. Dinner was delicious and the night quickly passed.

Horses saddled, we rode out of spike camp well before the hint of first light. Trusting the horses to guide us down the dark trail, Richard was intent on reaching our glassing spot as soon as possible.

The morning was calm and the lake smooth as glass. A starry night soon gave way to blue sky, but after an hour of glassing, we saw no sign of goats.

It was from here, along the shores of Tuchodi Lake, where we spotted several mountain goats, then began our relentless journey that covered over 3,000 vertical feet in a single day.

"They're up there," shared Richard, looking through the spotting scope. "We just have to go find them."

Tying off the horses, we soon shed our outer layers of clothes, filled the water bottles and cinched down the packs in preparation for the uphill journey. It took four hours of walking to break through the timber and rough country, to where we could start looking for goats.

On that uphill journey, it was encouraging seeing glimpses of mountain goat fur clinging to spruce tree limbs, tree trunks and rocks. No matter how hard I willed those goats to be down low in the timber, however, it just wasn't happening. Nonetheless, it was morally uplifting just to see sign that they had been there, no matter how many months prior it may have been.

Once we hit open terrain, the steepness of our climb dramatically increased. Our objective was to reach two areas where we'd seen goats moving the evening before. Mountain goats, especially mature billies, are very predictable in their daily routines this time of year. Richard felt confident that if we could make it to where we'd seen the goats the evening before, chances were high of their showing up in the same spot.

After another hour of intense hiking, we found what we were looking for, a white speck nearly two miles away in the bottom of a shaded, rocky canyon. Travis spotted him first, which isn't surprising. He's the best camera man I've ever worked with. Travis grew up hunting and has incredible eyes.

Five hours into the stalk we spotted our goat in the bottom of this canyon. Three hours later we were finally in shooting position.

He was a college wrestler and is young; his top physical shape knows no limits.

Travis had a bout of the flu on this trip, but kept pushing forward. An hour into the hike he ran out of water. Figuring we'd find a stream along the way, unfortunately for Travis, that didn't happen for another seven hours. I gave him sips of my water as needed, but I, too, was battling something only Travis knew about.

Four months earlier, while lifting weights, I tore a disk in my lower back. In this line of work, there is no down time, and my back didn't heal over the summer as I'd hoped. Now, here we were, on the toughest hunt of my life, and I was facing the most excruciating pain ever. The horseback rides were punishing, and now, with each and every step it felt like nails were being driven into my back.

It didn't help that we were side-hilling for hours, meaning the right side of my body took a constant beating on the short side of the hill. But I wasn't about to stop. I could tell Richard was growing frustrated, for our progress was slower than it should have been. He knew Travis was sick, and I told him I had a sore back, but that was the extent of it.

Three hours after spotting the goat, we still weren't anywhere near shooting range. By now my lower body was in constant, hot pain. Some steps felt as though a red-hot cattle prod was being driven into my legs and lower back. I can honestly say that at this point, if it wasn't for TV, I would have ended the hunt.

But the more I kept thinking about how far we'd come, and what a lifelong dream this hunt had been of mine, the more driven I became. I continually flashed back to those high school and college football days, where pushing myself to the physical and mental limits taught me so much about myself and how much I'm truly capable of. In high school I was a four sport letterman and quarterback and captain of the football team. Quitting in those situations was never an option, and it wasn't going to be on this hunt, either.

At times the pain was so excruciating, I honestly thought this might well be the last hunt of my life. But we pushed on. One time, Travis blacked out for a few minutes, but fortunately Richard had pushed ahead of us far enough not to see. This is where Travis' athletic background motivated him, too. Neither of us would quit until we finished the job.

It was hot, in the mid-60s, way above normal for early October in this northern portion of Canada. This was hard on our bodies, but good for hunting, as it forced goats into cooler, shaded spots.

12

Finally, four hours after first spotting the goat, we were in a position to judge how big he was. Up to this point, we weren't even sure if he was a shooter.

After studying the billy through the spotting scope, Richard put his horns at between 9 1/2- and 10-inches, which was what I'd always held as a standard in my mind. To tell you the truth, at this point I didn't care how big he was – if he was legal and had a good coat, that was all I wanted. I knew my body would not be able to make it up this mountain a second day in a row, period.

Though every moment of the hunt was special, it was tough. Stinging legs and burning lungs that begged for more air made me wish I'd have tried for a goat many years earlier in life, and with a healthy back. Bloodied fingers and torn fingernails, the result of grasping sharp rocks on the arduous climb, only added to the pain. I felt bad for Travis, carting that big camera, heavy tripod and a pack full of batteries and other hefty gear up the mountain. He didn't complain once. That kind of determination and sacrifice is tough to find in a person, let alone a talented camera man. At one point I told Travis he would never be allowed to be anyone else's full-time camera man, that we were partners from here on out. He smiled, which I know wasn't easy.

Making our final move to get in shooting position on the big billy, we pushed our bodies as hard as we could. Then the billy bedded down for a while, pinning us behind a lone spruce tree. Travis and I were thankful, for we needed the rest. By this time we were out of water, so the relief of the shade felt good.

When the goat got up, he started feeding our direction, and smiles washed across all our faces. A half-hour later and the billy was closer, now just inside 500 yards. Then he dropped into the creek bottom.

"Let's stay put, he'll come out right there," Richard pointed at the near ridge in front of us, where we saw the billy come out yesterday at this exact same time. "He'll be here, we just have to be patient," Richard encouraged.

After 45 minutes, our patience grew thin. We all knew the mountain goat should have come out long ago. We talked, thought, and talked some more. Then we all agreed to hike across the open hillside and try to find the goat, fearing he'd slipped up a draw we couldn't see from our position.

It was a risky move, for if we got busted while moving across the opening, there's no way we could have gotten the shot on film as things would have likely fallen apart too quickly. At the same time, if we sat and waited, and the goat didn't show, we'd be out a day of valued hunting, and I knew there was no coming back.

In eight hours we'd climbed over 3,000 vertical feet in elevation, the most Richard had ever climbed for a goat in a single day. We only had a couple hundred more feet to go, then we'd be able to see where the billy went.

Gathering packs, spotting scopes and camera gear, we poked our heads from behind the spruce tree we'd been hiding behind, and there he was. Glowing larger than life, a stunning, white mass of a goat, stood in the exact spot where Richard said he'd come out.

His heavy frame and muscular shoulder hump caught me off-guard. He appeared larger than I'd anticipated. Given his immense, blocky stature, he also seemed much closer than the 163 yards the Nikon rangefinder registered.

Slowly, quietly, we hunkered back down behind the tree. Slipping the rifle off my shoulder and the pack from my back, I soon had a solid rest. Then the wind changed. "He's smelling us," urged Richard. "Take him now!"

But I didn't have a clear shot at his chest through the tall grass he stood in. Then he lifted his nose higher into the wind, and turned a fraction to the right, exposing his vitals. That was all I needed.

Placing the amber dot of the Trijicon crosshair behind the billy's shoulder, I calmed my nerves and pressured the trigger on the .300 Winchester Magnum. The shot surprised me, but when the goat folded on the spot, a wave of emotions shot through my body. My mountain goat dreams had just become reality.

Approaching the gorgeous animal, his long, pure white pelage found me speechless. He'd tumbled over 50 yards down a steep, rocky cliff, so when Richard pulled his 10-inch horns out of the rocks, both fully in-tact, the silence was broken with cheers of joy. He was a brute of a goat, surpassing even my wildest dreams.

The best part, he came to rest mere feet from a cool, fresh, rushing stream. Before snapping a couple hundred photos, we all dunked our filtered water bottles and drank to the point of feeling sick. We had gone too long without water, and were in desperate need of hydration.

Travis was unquestionably sick, and I was in immense pain. But the victory of the hunt, and the fact it was all captured on film for Trijicon's Game Chasers, on the Outdoor Channel, made for the best pain killer imaginable.

What the camera's didn't show, however, were the hours of work that followed. Though we quickly skinned the goat for a lifesize mount, and boned out the meat in a timely fashion, we still had to get off the mountain.

Spike camp, a place we didn't see much of during this goat hunt.

Travis continued packing his heavy load, along with some meat, while I tossed the hide and some more meat into my pack. Richard took the bulk of the meat in his pack, along with some other loose gear. Richard's pack later weighed in just over 90 pounds, mine at 80, and Travis' a little under that.

Hiking off that mountain, darkness consumed us in the most treacherous part. With nearly 300 vertical feet of sheer rock between us and the giant boulders in the creek bottom below, we carefully placed each step we took. One missed stride, one stumble, would mean certain death. This was not where we planned on being at this point in the day.

After tediously picking our way across the rocky mountainside, we soon found ourselves in the middle of low-growing brush that tangled our feet with every stride. The terrain was still extremely steep, and for every five steps I took, I tripped, tumbled and moaned in pain from the shock delivered to my back.

My legs were numbed to the point of not working like my mind instructed them. Every time I hit the ground, my body coiled in anticipation of the blow. There were no muscle relaxers strong enough to dull the excruciating pain I was now feeling.

Travis was doing better; I was holding up the progress. When we hit the heavy timber, I pleaded with Richard to stop and spend the night in the soft, thick moss-covered floor. He denied, pointing out that though it was 10:00 p.m. now and the stars were out, that could all change in a short time.

The toughest hunt of my life was rewarded with this incredible, record-class mountain goat. Never have my physical and mental limits been pushed to the extreme like they were on this demanding excursion.

We rested, drank more water and pushed on. By now, both of my feet were numb, not from my back pain, but form the physical beating they took. Tripping over limbs, logs and thick moss, it was a challenge to maintain a positive mental state. Then I just had to think back on the rewards of this great hunt I'd experienced mere hours ago.

It was midnight by the time we reached the horses, where we tied them 14 hours earlier. We were elated to see all three horses still there. Dropping our packs, we removed our boots and socks and soaked our aching feet in the ice-cold waters of Tuchodi Lake.

We'd come full-circle. The evening before, we were skipping rocks on this beautiful lake, anticipating the goat hunt the following day. Now, I was in the most pain I'd ever felt, soaking my weary body parts in the same lake, right where we'd spotted my goat from the evening prior.

The last thing I felt like doing was slipping into the saddle, riding a horse back to spike camp. However, my back felt so shredded, my loss of leg control so great, I had no choice.

Letting the horses blindly guide us through darkness, it was a gratifying feeling reflecting back on what we'd accomplished on this day, October 2, 2008. Staring at millions of silver stars glistening in the black, night sky above, I couldn't help but wonder how my wife, Tiffany, was doing on this, her birthday.

Arriving in camp at 2:00 a.m., the wrangler hopped out of his bedroll and had the saddle off my horse before I made it to the campfire. Soon, a hot meal followed with plenty more to drink, then we slept.

The next morning found us back in the saddle, headed for base camp. On occasion I'd catch glimpses of the granite peaks where my goat, the king of the mountain, had lived his entire life. It was a bitter-sweet feeling. I ended up losing three toenails, and the tops of both of my feet were numb for several months following the hunt. I wished my body would have been running on all cylinders so I could have experienced the full pleasure of such a demanding hunt.

Then again, it was gratifying to know just how far we as hunters can push ourselves, and what we are physically and mentally capable of enduring to turn our dreams into reality. It's moments like this, that no matter how hard we try, we simply can't explain to the non-hunters of the world just how passionate we are about what we love to do. That's hunting, and I can't imagine living life without it.

Chapter 2:

Growing A Hunter

For every adult, their most memorable hunt is usually their own.
But once your child takes their first big game animal,
that all changes.

As the herd of pronghorns broke over the horizon, heading our way, we sat still as stone statues. Braxton, my six year old son, had his bipod already set, gun shouldered, waiting for a shot opportunity .

The herd continued forward, unaware of our presence. At 75 yards they paused and fed, but the buck was in the middle of the bunch, covered by a pair of does. With the bright Texas sun starting to rise in the background, I grew nervous.

"Would all those months, years, of practice be blown by something we hadn't factored in, shooting into direct light?" I wondered. "Was Braxton nervous, or had his previous four years of shooting been enough to give him the confidence he needed to make this shot?" We were about to find out.

Though we call Oregon home, the beaver state was among 20 states in the nation at the time that had age restrictions on hunters, which explains why we turned to Texas for Braxton's first big game experience. Texas, on the other hand, was one of 30 states who had youth- and family-friendly hunting laws. What's more, according to the National Shooting Sports Foundation (NSSF), 17 of these states had no restrictions on youth hunters, meaning parents, not politics, were the ones deciding when their child was ready to hunt.

So why is it then, that the number of hunters participating in the sport of hunting continues to decline? There are several reasons, really. One of the biggest obstacles is the mandatory coursework required to obtain a certified hunting license. This, in itself, costs time, something Americans are lacking during this day and age of two-parent working households and single-parent homes.

But what's more shocking – according to data compiled by the NSSF – only 25% of youth who live in hunting households, are active in the sport. At the time of Braxton's 2006 hunt, over the past 25 years the number of hunters in the United States had dropped 23%. Not only are youth restrictions likely compounding the decline of active hunters, but new hunters, no matter what their age, are not joining the sport like they used to.

Though Braxton's hunt took place at an early age, we began preparing for it prior to his second birthday. He started by shooting a BB gun, with close parental supervision. At age two, he was proficiently shooting a .22, and started shooting a recurve bow. By age four he could load and operate various models of .22s, on his own, again with close supervision. It's amazing what a child is capable of doing if given the opportunity.

We started by shooting off a solid bench at paper targets in the back yard. If you don't live in the countryside, a shooting range is the next best bet for gaining practical shooting practice. But youngsters can grow tired of punching paper, so we spiced up things by introducing balloons, cans, plastic bottles filled with water and clay pigeons hung on a board. Being able to see targets break upon bullet impact greatly increases interest in children.

The next progression came at the age of four, where Braxton, and his younger brother, Kazden (age two), took to eastern Oregon on a varmint shoot for Belding's ground squirrels. With the aid of a portable shooting bench, both boys could load, locate varmints in their scope and execute shots with their .22s out to 50 yards. The key here was getting the kids into a rifle that fit their short statures. If kids aren't comfortable shooting, they won't like it as much, nor will they develop and hone necessary skills to improve as their bodies mature.

When we decided to take Braxton on his pronghorn hunt, he was five years old, and we had nearly a year to prepare for it. This gave us time to learn the animal's anatomy and study its behavior. Together we read numerous stories on hunting pronghorns, and studied books on shot placement. We also watched several videos during the course of the year, learning how these flighty animals behave. All of this taught Braxton what he needed to know about shot placement as well as when to take the proper shot.

On other big game animals that I'd taken, Braxton was with me during the field dressing process, and was able to see where the vitals of a big game animal are located, what they look like and learn their functions. Whether it's your child or someone else's, this is a valuable science lesson to be learned on a real level, not just off paper.

As far as the shooting progression, at this point Braxton was ready to shoot off sticks. He wasn't strong enough to hold his rifle and shoot offhand, so we knew his shot would come from a stationary position, off a bipod, or would not come at all. The animal would also have to be standing broadside in order for the small, fast-flying bullet to do its job. Texas allows any center-fire cartridge to be used on big game, and Braxton was shooting a .204.

During the last four months of his shooting, Braxton concentrated on paper targets that we painted to look like a pronghorn. We crafted a model of his Trijicon scope reticle and physically went over precisely where it was to be positioned on the buck in order for him to take a shot. Braxton also made a pronghorn collage that he hung by his bed. Each night he took a small model of his scope reticle and placed it on each animal's vitals. This was invaluable practice through repetition, and taught him exactly where to put his bullet.

In order to maximize a steady form while shooting, Braxton sat cross-legged, elbows on both knees, left hand curled beneath his chin, holding the butt of his rifle (he's right handed). This maximized the number of anchor points, whereby eliminating shake. For the last year, he did all of his shooting on a Thompson-Center G2 frame. He progressed from a .22 barrel to a .17 and .204. The .25-06 had too much recoil for him, so we set that aside for another year. I liked the prospects of teaching Braxton how to handle a gun with a single-shot rifle. Not only did this teach him the importance of making that first shot count, it also kept him focused and calm.

During the week he'd fire over 100 rounds through his .22, some through

To better familiarize Braxton with his Trijicon scope and shot placement on a pronghorn, we made a model of his reticle. Next, we crafted several targets showing the animal's external anatomy, and where the shot would need to be placed.

his .17 and a few through the .204. As long as he was hitting good with his .204, I was happy, for his repetition and form development came from shooting his .22. We kept a Limbsaver recoil pad on his stock at all times, in order to not only absorb the shock from his .204, but to allow him to get used to the feel, no matter what caliber he shot. His Trijicon scope allowed him to shoot with both eyes open, a good technique to learn at such a young age. From the time he started shooting a rifle, this was the only scope Braxton ever looked through.

Utilizing multiple anchor points while putting in range-time, Braxton was able to achieve a rock-steady rest. When it came time for the hunt, he was very well prepared and confident of his ability to make the shot.

Finally, Braxton practiced from several seated positions, out to 200 yards. From shooting uphill, downhill, off two knees, one knee and seated, once he got a good grouping from all positions, he was ready for the hunt.

We arrived in Texas a day early, so we could scout with good friend and outfitter, Cal Ferguson of 4F Outfitters. Braxton got to look at dozens of pronghorns, including some nice bucks as we cruised the northern deserts of Texas. He also laid eyes on country far different than that where we lived.

That night Braxton was excited for the opening morning of antelope season. Once he met the five other hunters in camp, all adults, he really felt privileged.

It didn't take long until we spotted the first herd of pronghorns early in the morning. Closer inspection revealed a good buck, one worth trying for.

Wanting to do it right, Cal and I agreed to go spot and stalk, or nothing. We wanted Braxton's first hunting experience to be one where a well thought-out plan followed by a stealthy stalk, would result in a good shooting opportunity. Our plan worked.

As the herd of pronghorns continued feeding to our right, along a knoll, they entered into some long grass. Braxton had to shift from his seated position to his knees and readjust his bipod. After settling in, he still felt good about the shot angle. "The sun's okay, I can see the buck really good," he assured me, his cheek pressed firmly into the gun.

At the age of six, Braxton took this Texas pronghorn, his first big game animal. All of his practice paid off in the form of a perfect stalk and a one shot kill. As a father, I couldn't have been more proud.

Now 100 yards away from us, it was obvious we had to make something happen before the herd fed out of sight. As Braxton pulled back the hammer on his Thompson-Center .204, I grunted, and the buck stopped. The moment his wide, sweeping horns turned our way and his body shifted broadside, Braxton centered the scope behind the buck's shoulder and let loose. The shot was absolutely perfect, a double-lung hit.

The buck ran 30 yards and piled up. It was the most rewarding hunt of my life, for my son had just taken his first big game animal. All of the preparation came down to one shot, and Braxton connected. The best part, we caught it all on film for a television episode of Outdoor America, which I used to cohost on the Outdoor Channel. As if the pressure of a first big game hunt wasn't enough, Braxton achieved his goal with TV camera hovering over his shoulder. Then again, he was really too young to fully understand the true pressures of TV. To him it was all fun, and now we had some great eating meat to take home.

It's a proven fact that youth who start hunting at an early age are more likely to hunt as adults. The key is getting them started, now. Hunting is more than a pastime. It's our culture and defines who many of us are. It enriches our lives beyond what can be learned in any formal setting. It's a freedom and an honor we as Americans are blessed to have.

Thanks to this Texas pronghorn hunting experience, a seed was planted in Braxton. I can only pray this seed germinates into a lifelong passion of hunting and spending time in the outdoors. There's no better way I know of building bonds than in the field, working to achieve a common goal, together.

Chapter 3:

Blacktail Hugs & Tears

I love hunting any animal, with any weapon,
but if I had one day left to hunt, it would be spent pursuing the
Columbia blacktail deer.

Darkness fell fast in the little draw we hunted, but we didn't give up hope. "Let's just wait a few more minutes," encouraged Parrey Cremeans. Like me, Parrey's most passionate about his blacktails, so he didn't have to tell me twice.

Minutes later, two dark shadows appeared from under the oak trees. When they slithered into an opening, it was easy to see they were both does, but it was the way they moved that caught our attention.

"They're being pushed by a buck," Parrey whispered. That exact thought crossed my mind, but the fact it was October 20th, and given that it was over 90° earlier in the day, it didn't seem right.

Then a bigger form emerged from beneath the oaks. You could tell by the stature it was a mature buck, but not until I looked at him through my Trijicon scope did I realize how big he was. With a tall, deep-forked rack spanning past his ear tips, it was one of the largest blacktails I'd ever laid eyes on.

We were losing light fast, but I couldn't break away from the fact the giant buck was dogging the does, stopping to lip-curl where one had just urinated. Snapping his head down, he followed the does and chased them around an oak, and out of sight. I thought I'd lost my chance, then they darted into another clearing, moving uphill.

When the buck stopped and lip-curled one more time, followed by some rub-urinating, I moved the safety to off and took the shot. At just under 200 yards, it should have been a slam-dunk, but I missed. I quickly chambered another round, shot and missed again. Both shots missed to the right. There were no excuses, I just flat out blew it.

Here I was, hunting my favorite big game animal, and I'd just missed a shot at the biggest blacktail buck I'd ever looked at through a scope. I was livid with myself, for I had dismally failed.

Cremeans tried offering words of encouragement, but it didn't help. I knew what caliber of buck I'd just missed and that rarely, if ever, does a blacktail hunter get a second chance at a trophy animal like that. Cremeans' knew it too.

I've been fortunate to hunt many exciting places around the globe, and I'm convinced that some of the best hunters I've spent time with are those hard-core, accomplished blacktail hunters. These are the folks who consistently take big bucks, and who know deer behavior inside and out. They're also the ones who can track and read sign exceptionally well, and who are willing to hike high into the hills, or deep into the coastal rainforest in search of their quarry, no matter how rugged or miserable the conditions.

Within the first few minutes of ever hunting with Cremeans, I knew I'd found a new hunting partner. The stealth which he moved, the way he interpreted sign and the focus he maintained made me feel like I was outside my skin, watching myself. It's this kind of dedication that cuts off all else that's happening in the world, and puts you in the realm of blacktails. It's this level of commitment that's necessary every second you're in the blacktail woods if you want to secure a trophy class buck.

On this hunt I joined Cremeans on land he's hunted since boyhood, very near Redding, California. One look at the record books and it's obvious what a dominant presence northern California has in their pages. These are the caliber of animals that really get me pumped up. These are the big bucks I like pursuing, as does Cremeans.

A year, almost to the day of my hunt, Parrey hunted an area just east of us. On that day he spotted what appeared to be a good buck from high atop a ridge. Stalking his way down the hill, Cremeans lost sight of the buck, but knew the general area where he'd last seen him.

Slowing his approach, Parrey scoured the brushline, every shadow and the tall grass. Relying on a grove of oak trees for cover, he moved from one fat trunk to another, searching for the buck. Realizing he'd gone too far, Parrey felt he'd blown it, obviously having walked past the buck.

But Parrey didn't give up. Instead, he moved slowly back up the hill, glassing every bit of ground as he inched forward. The wind was perfect, though the going slow due to dry leaves and grass that crunched beneath every step.

Then Parrey caught glimpse of an antler tine. It was immersed in yellow grass, pointing straight into the sky. Still unsure of the buck's size, Parrey was prepared to wait and let the buck wake up from his morning nap, undisturbed. Then the wind shifted and Parrey knew he had to do something, fast.

Intentionally stepping on a twig, the crack made the buck throw up his head, and when he did, Cremeans fought the urge to look at his rack. "I knew he was big, and that's all that mattered," relived Parrey. "At about 40 yards, there was no time to think, just react."

In reflex action, Cremeans centered the crosshairs of his scope on the only place he could see – the buck's neck. At the shot, the buck's head dropped. Obscured, once again by the tall, yellow grass, Parrey had no idea what he had until he actually stood over the mammoth buck.

High, heavy tines sprawled every direction. It was at that moment Cremeans realized he'd just taken the true buck of a lifetime.

Parrey's inland blacktail sported an eye-popping 31 1/8-inch spread, and carried a massive, 9x10 rack with impressive eye guards. After a 60 day drying period, Parrey's buck taped out at 198 7/8-inches and surely would have gone over 200-inches, green.

Like the region where Parrey took his buck, the one I hunted with him was also known to hold migratory deer that move in from the hills east of

Parrey Cremeans took this giant inland Columbia blacktail near Redding, California. Parrey has been hunting this land his whole life and knows it, and the animals, extremely well.

town. The migration here is not spurred by harsh weather, rather a lack of food due to high temperatures.

"It gets so arid in the hills of this area, all the food sources dry up, forcing the deer to lower elevations," noted Parrey. "When the deer move into this area, acorns, buck brush and grass become valued food sources."

But there are also resident populations of blacktails where I was hunting, much lower in the valley with year-round food and water, than where Parrey took his magnum buck. In fact, Parrey had been doing his homework, and first laid eyes on the buck I wanted nearly two months prior to my arrival.

The benefit of hunting this section of northern California is the openness of the land, where a resident buck can be seen on more than one occasion. Where I grew up hunting blacktails in the timber-choked brush country of western Oregon, catching a glimpse of a trophy buck on more than one occasion is almost unheard of, despite the fact they live and die within a very small area.

In early September, Parrey spotted the buck a second time, mere yards from where he'd first seen him. Then, a few weeks after that, one of Parrey's clients had the buck walk out of the brush and stand broadside at 50 yards. The hunter locked-up with buck fever and never fired a shot. That worked out well for me.

With our sights still set on the big buck, the second morning of my hunt found us in the same area. Though we didn't see our buck, we did see other bucks, including two very good ones I would have taken in a second were it not for the fact I had a score to settle. Both of these big bucks were chasing does, and one's neck was so inflated, you'd have thought it was mid-November.

We stuck it out until late morning, then took a lunch break when the mercury hit 90°. That evening, nothing moved, not even a doe.

Had I blown the buck out of there with my missed shots? Did he take off in search of more does in heat? Did our mere presence force him into thick cover? A million questions raced through my mind, and there was no solace. Fact was I'd blown a key chance at a trophy buck, and could only pray I'd get a second shot. Sleep was almost nonexistent those two nights, as I grew more upset with myself.

The following morning began anew. Temperatures were forecast to soar into the mid-90s, so we hit it early. Rather than slowly hunt our way into the target area, we hoofed it in in the dark. By first light we were where we wanted to be.

As dawn broke, two does moved down through some oak trees, followed by a big bodied buck. Tree limbs blocked our view, but given his location we wasted no time closing the gap a bit more.

From the minute I set foot in the woods with Parrey Cremeans, I knew I'd found a new hunting partner. His level of knowledge, dedication and determination are unmatched by few men I've hunted with.

Minutes later we were 150 yards from where we'd last seen the deer. Just as we settled in, the does moved across a clearing, and the buck followed. A quick look through the binoculars confirmed he was the buck we wanted, the one I'd missed two days prior.

Heart pounding, palms sweating, nerves growing more tense, it all seemed like a dream to me. The second chance I'd hoped for was unfolding before us.

But as the does moved into a thicket, the buck quickly followed. He squirted through the opening so fast, I couldn't get a shot. Anticipating the deer would come out the bottom, we moved 30 yards farther down the hill.

From where we now sat, we could see every escape route surrounding the half-acre of brush the deer had vanished in. Question was, where would they come out? Or would they stay there and bed for the day?

Minutes slowly passed, then the does quickly slithered out the bottom. By the way they walked, it was obvious they were being pushed by a rut-crazed buck. Swinging the rifle on the shooting sticks, I was more than ready.

"Here he comes," Cremeans eagerly whispered. "He's coming out right on the same trail the does did." The excitement in Parrey's voice jacked me up another notch.

A quick reading on the rangefinder revealed just over 100 yards. I picked out an opening between the brushline and a large bolder in the bottom of the dry creekbed. If the buck followed the same path as the does, moving left to right, he'd walk right into my scope.

"I'm on him," whispered Travis Ralls, my camera man. That was the only confirmation I needed to hear.

When the buck reached the exact point I was holding on, I put the dot of the Trijicon duplex scope on the kill zone. There was no time to waste, for another stride or two and the buck would be swallowed-up by more brush. It was now or never.

At the shot, the buck dropped on the spot. He didn't so much as flinch a single muscle. I was so overcome with excitement and sheer joy, I think I even gave Cremeans a big hug and a peck on the cheek. The next few minutes were all a blur, and my entire body started to tremble. There are few animals that do that to me, and a blacktail of this caliber is one of them.

Making sure the animal wasn't going anywhere, I was speechless as I stared at his massive rack through the scope. "You ready to go see him?" asked Parrey. "Give me a minute," I replied.

It was obvious the buck was down for good, so I took a quick break to walk to the top of the hill and phone my wife. As soon as I heard her voice I started to tremble. The words wouldn't come out. I gasped, hesitated, and squeaked out, "I got him!" She new what I was talking about, for I'd spent many counseling sessions on the phone with her since I first missed this buck two days prior. I could feel tears of joy running down my cheeks.

"I have the best job in the world, you know," I stuttered between breaths. "I could never imagine doing anything else for a living...you know that?" In her always supportive nature, she replied, "I love you, now go get your deer."

Approaching the downed Columbia blacktail, there was no question he was the biggest I'd taken in my life, to date. A perfectly symmetrical 4x4 with solid eye guards, he measured 152 5/8-inches.

My prayers had been answered and I got a second chance. But that was the last animal I shot with that gun. Though I cleanly killed the buck at barely over 100 yards, my shot hit him in the neck, way right of where I was aiming. My heart sank when I thought of what the results could have been had that buck been moving from right to left. A definite gut shot, likely a wounded deer. I couldn't take that.

My best Columbia blacktail to date. This 152 5/8" record book buck was the result of persistence and team work, which made the final outcome even more special.

When I got home and shot the gun again, it was shooting to the right exactly nine inches at 100 yards. That explained why I missed the buck the first time. Obviously, I'd shot the gun and had it dialed in prior to the hunt, but I could never get it zeroed back in to my liking. I lost confidence in that gun and never fired it again.

In more than 30 years of hunting blacktails, I can count on two fingers the times I've received a second chance – it's simply rare with these cagey creatures.

Through hard work, patience and persistence, redemption came on this California blacktail hunt. Of course, it wouldn't have happened were it not for the efforts of my new hunting buddy, Parrey Cremeans. That's just one of the many rewards blacktail hunters earn; new friendships with devoted hunters who share the same deep passion that courses through your veins 365 days a year.

Chapter 4:

Big Money Bull

Working as a full-time television host has many advantages, not the least of which is the opportunity to go on high-end hunts that would otherwise remain only a dream. This is one of those hunts.

A $10,000 commissioner's tag to hunt any elk in Wyoming during the November rifle season. That's what one sponsor treated me to in 2008.

From a business perspective, it made logical sense. The company, who will remain anonymous, wanted their gear featured in harsh conditions, going after the highest profile big game animal in North America, the Rocky Mountain elk.

In a nationwide survey I'd read not too long before the trip, hunters across the country were asked what their number one dream hunt in America would be. The most popular answer was the Rocky Mountain elk.

The company behind this tag looked forward to having the TV show, but knew I'd generate magazine articles from it, providing further exposure. In addition, they intended to use the images from the hunt on national print advertising campaigns, posters, their website and more.

Five years ago, this kind of hunt would have made me incredibly nervous. The fact someone would entrust me to hunt a trophy bull on a tag that they paid for is flattering, and now that I've been in the business for several years, I believe it's a good move on their part. But there's still a part of me that struggles with such commitments.

Growing up hunting on public lands, unguided, was all I knew until getting into this industry. In hind sight, those more than 30 years of solo experience were invaluable, and helped pave the way to where I am today.

In today's competitive marketing world, outfitters, booking agencies, guides and hunting related companies are seeking high-profile attention to help boost their business. I've been blessed to be presented with some very special hunts, from a $50,000 African lion hunt to more than half that for red stag hunts in New Zealand, to elk, moose, brown bears and other glamor species that carry a lofty price tag.

Believe me, on hunts like this, or any hunts for that matter, I count my blessings each and every moment, and thank the good Lord for putting me in a position to carry out such responsibilities. Though it's hunting, at this level it's very much a job.

At first, I didn't really like the proposition of hunting on other people's dime, but now it's become a normal part of the job. I've never had precious things handed to me such as high-dollar hunts, but if it wasn't for where my career is now, I would not be hunting these great animals. That's why I feel so compelled to share these stories with the rest of the world. If it weren't for this line of business, these hunts would be beyond my reach.

I'm often asked, "How do you get so many tags each year?" It's simple, really. I usually apply for more than 20 out of state, hard-to-draw hunts every year. Of these I might draw one or two tags. From there, I sort through the many invitations from outfitters, to hunt with them on landowner permits or outfitter sponsored tags. After that, I fill holes with over-the-counter tags to round out the rest of the filming season, then see where sponsors might step in and offer further support.

At this level, hunting is business and I represent companies, outfitters, television channels and production companies based on my success and work ethics. My formal education background and decades of real hunting experience are strengths I try to capitalize on when building a quality TV show every time I'm in the field. I know I'm not the best host on television, but I try my best to educate viewers. I'm not an entertainer like some hosts, but feel I can hold my own with any of them when it comes to true, hard-core hunting, knowing animal behavior and having outdoor knowledge. The pressure to produce can be overwhelming at times, especially when things don't go as anticipated. This Wyoming elk was one of those hunts.

On this hunt I teamed up with one of the state's best known bighorn sheep guides, Justin Jarrett, of Wapiti Ridge Outfitters. Justin had guided several commissioner and governor tag elk hunters in recent years, and like me, was confident we'd have a crack at a big bull.

We chose to hunt Unit 58, just southwest of Cody, Wyoming. My best boyhood friend, Tom Buller, lives in Cody, and a few years prior, his daughter

The hardest part of filming outdoor television shows is finding a top-notch camera man. I've had some good ones and not so good ones over the years. Travis Ralls, pictured here, is the hardest working, most dedicated videographer I've worked with. We've shared many pains, struggles and ultimate highs, together.

drew this prized tag. I went along on that hunt, and every day we saw bulls in the 375-inch range. We also saw a handful that would have went into the upper 390s. We saw over 20 big bulls each day, and that's what we hoped for on my hunt.

For Justin and I, we had our sights set on a 390-inch bull or bigger. Hunting off horseback, we figured we'd be able to get the job done in two to three days. After day five, we were more than nervous.

We both had a lot on the line. Justin was wanting to get a show for his outfitting business, as did I, but I also had that $10,000 tag looming over my head. I'd already cancelled another elk hunt because this one took longer than planned, and was within a day of having to cancel a mule deer hunt in Montana.

On the first day of the hunt, we were hit hard with snow, which was perfect. However, by early afternoon the snow was all gone, and that was the last we'd see of it. We watched a few small bulls that first day, but nothing over 320-inches.

Day two found us on the south side of the unit, and though we saw over 20 bulls, none were big enough to get excited about. On the third day, we caught a herd just as they fed into the timber. We made a decision to wait for those elk to move out of the trees, given the fact we weren't able to get a good look at all the animals. We didn't want to leave elk to find elk, so we waited.

It's worth pointing out that hunting for TV is much different than hunting for myself. Had I been hunting alone, I'd have slowly picked my way through the timber, tried finding a bull and shot him, likely as he was moved away. Chances are, my view of him would be in dark shadows, thick brush

With the aid of horses, we were able to get into prime elk county in Wyoming's Unit 58. We just couldn't find the trophy bull we wanted.

and he'd be spooked. None of those elements make for quality TV, which is why we chose to wait out the elk, hoping they'd naturally move into an opening where we could capture them on film and get a clear shot.

The thing we were up against on day two and three was bad weather. Actually, it was good weather, but bad for us. It was so unseasonably warm, the elk were only staying in the open during the first and last few minutes of daylight, literally. During the day, absolutely no animals were moving.

Hunkering behind a couple giant boulders on that third day, we waited for the elk to leave the timber. By noon, nothing had budged and we knew we were in for a long day. Then the wind kicked up. Sustained winds in excess of 40 miles per hour lasted until dark, and the elk never left the timber. The hunt was quickly escalating into one of the most frustrating either of us had been on. I was starting to feel the pressure.

I'd applied for this elk tag in the past, but a nonresident has just about as good of a chance of pulling a bighorn tag as landing this one. So, to have a commissioner's tag in my pocket, I was more than confident we'd get a big bull. After day three, I was beginning to wonder.

Day four found us on the northern fringes of the unit. Tom Buller and one of his buddies pitched in. Between all of us, we covered more land on that day than on the three previous days combined. We saw only a few elk here and there, and very little sign.

Day five found us back on the eastern side of the unit, glassing the timberlines where we'd seen the highest concentration of bulls. By this time, the local hunters who held tags had reached the same conclusion we did as to where the bulls were, and we saw over a dozen hunters on this day. We did see the odd bull here and there, but nothing to get excited about.

On day six, we were in the saddle earlier than any other morning. Since the bulls were melting into the timber so quickly after first light, Justin wanted to get as far as we could into the many draws of the deepest, hardest to access patches of timber. My backside was getting saddle sore by this time, and the torn disc I'd been nursing in my lower back didn't help things.

After bumping a bull in the first patch of timber we crossed, we decided to wait. It was too dark to shoot, but we could see it was a bull. We didn't want to risk spooking any others, so we sat, waiting for more light to appear on the horizon.

As daylight slowly came, we glassed from the top of the next ridge, where Justin spotted the biggest bull of the hunt. He'd go all of 360, and we wasted no time putting the move on him. Just as we made it to the bull, we saw his backside vanish into the timber. That quickly our best opportunity faded away without my even shouldering the rifle.

Hiking back to the horses, we rode up to the next ridge and glassed another timberline. A 350-inch bull glowed as the sun topped the ridge and illuminated his yellow coat. Then a bigger bull stepped out. "He's a solid 7x7 that will easily go over 375", Justin whispered excitedly as he peered through the spotting scope.

Here we were, into our sixth day of hunting and this was the biggest bull we'd seen. Actually, the three bulls we'd seen on this morning were the three biggest of the trip. On a normal year, we should have been passing up bulls like this all day long.

As happened the previous days, the temperatures warmed up quickly and the bulls wasted no time feeding into the timber. Where we'd seen the big bull was well over a mile away, but we decided to ride the horses to that point and wait him out.

By noon, three other hunters rode through the very timber the bull sought seclusion in. By 2:00 p.m., another pair of hunters would ride through the same timber patch. Our spirits dropped as the perils of dealing with many hunters on this public access piece of ground was making it tough to get the TV show we sought.

An hour before dark, way off in the distance, three bulls fed out of the timber. They were too far to reach by nightfall, and thankfully, were not shooters.

Then a herd of about 20 cows and calves appeared in another open meadow. This was the earliest we'd seen elk move. Our positive spirits were returning.

With about an hour of daylight remaining, we were settled in, glassing, from the highest point on the northeast side of the unit. Then Justin caught glimpse of a herd as they moved into the bottom of the valley we were watching.

Though the herd was low in elevation, and we could see a couple respectable bulls, it was too brushy to tell exactly what we were dealing with. Decision time. Do we leave the area and chance that there's a big bull in the herd, or do we wait, hoping more elk appear before us?

"These elk are about as close as we're going to get 'em," Justin noted, "and we still have to cover a half-mile to reach them." He had a point. Though we were sitting on a good vantage point, we were running out of daylight. Given the location of the herd, we decided to take a chance and go for it.

Hopping on the horses, we trotted down the back side of the hill, then ran through a brushy creek bottom toward where the elk were heading. Our intent was to cut them off in the last patch of mixed spruce and aspen trees.

When we broke out into the first meadow, we figured we had another 400 yards to go. Then we saw a lone cow. She saw us, too. In the fading light, however, she couldn't tell what we were. Slowly, we slithered off the horses, left them standing in the middle of the meadow, and used their bodies as cover to sneak back into the brush we'd just ridden through. It worked, and soon we were quietly jogging up a wooded draw, trying to close the distance before dark.

From this exact spot, Justin Jarrett located the bull we finally ended up getting. Justin is a hard working, talented outfitter, whom I'd hunt with anywhere, anytime.

Three hundred yards from the herd, Justin spotted two bulls. One was okay, a 320 bull, the other a bit bigger, pushing 340-inches.

"What do you want to do," Justin asked. Looking at the bull through the binoculars, his impressive high, long-tined rack looked good to me. "Kill him," I replied.

We had five minutes of filming light left.

When Travis, my camera man, knew of my decision, he turned on the camera. It wasn't working. This was our 13th hunt of the fall, and it was the first malfunction we had with the camera. He turned it off and back on again. Still, nothing.

Because we'd left the horses so quickly, all Travis' gear was still strapped to his horse. What's that saying, "Whatever can go wrong, will go wrong," or something to that effect. Now we were down to three minutes of filming light.

Justin and I sought cover in the creek bottom and ran closer to the herd. I told Travis to try and fix the camera, then catch up with us, that I'd already be in the shooting sticks, ready to cut loose the moment he showed up.

Erecting the shooting sticks, elk started shuffling by, single file, 150 yards from us. Two minutes later, Travis was by my side, camera rolling. "How'd you fix it," I whispered in surprise. "Prayer," he smiled.

Instantly, Travis got on the bull and gave me the green light to shoot. Then the bull stopped behind a spruce tree. With only moments of shooting light remaining, the bull, the last one in the herd, finally walked into the open. He had no idea we were there.

Placing the glowing apex of the Trijicon scope behind the bull's shoulder, I was amazed by how much light the device gathered. It, along with the tripod shooting sticks, made connecting on the shot simple. Pulling the trigger on my Thompson Center Icon, chambered in .300 Winchester Magnum, the bullet punched a hole through both lungs of the bull. An insurance shot anchored the bull and eliminated any tracking job in the dark.

As we walked toward the fallen bull, Justin looked back in the meadow where we'd left the horses. They were nowhere to be seen. The rifle shots had obviously spooked them. Since we had no time and no place to tie them off, the question was, how far did the horses run?

While Justin ran to find the horses, Travis and I went to take care of the bull. Like Travis, I left my pack on the horse. It had all my gear in it, from knives to flashlights to warm clothes, food and matches. I did have a small, two-inch blade pocket knife, and that's what I field dressed the bull with. Not ideal, but it worked.

What worried me was spending the night out there, for we had no survival gear between the three of us. Though the daytime temperatures were near 70°, the nighttime temperatures would drop into the 'teens. We were not prepared for this, and in our haste to get a TV show, we made some poor decisions come crunch time, leaving our gear on the horses.

Fortunately, Travis had a headlamp in his pocket and it worked well for gutting the bull. Justin had no light. As Travis and I finished our job, we heard a horse blow through his nose. Never had I been more comforted by such a sound. Miraculously, Justin had found all three horses, together, nearly a mile from where we'd left them.

Riding the horses out in the pitch dark, through bogs, across creeks, over blown down trees and through thick timber was not what I'd call fun, but knowing that we'd worked so hard and come away with a show, it was gratifying. It wasn't until after 10:00 p.m. that we made it back to the rig and got the horses taken care of. We returned the next morning to finish butchering and packing out the bull.

Was the bull all we'd hoped for? Obviously not, not when the hunt began. But several variables changed, and all were against us. That's hunting,

Not until I started shooting television shows did I realize the difference a solid set of shooting sticks could make. At this level, I can't afford to miss, and a good gun, scope and shooting stick – I prefer a tripod – can make all the difference in accuracy. These tools played a big part on this hunt.

Our efforts finally paid off with this hard-won bull. For a better look at this Wyoming elk, check out the cover of this book.

and if I had to do it all over again, I wouldn't change a thing. Though the bull was a good 50-inches shy of what we had our sights set on, he was a dandy bull, nonetheless. In fact, I was so proud of that bull, all he represented and how hard we worked for him, that he graces the cover of this very book.

It's worth noting that, not until I started filming TV shows did I use tripod style shooting sticks on my hunts. Now I won't head into the field without one. The stability and accuracy these tools offer make connecting on a high percentage of shots very real. I'm often asked why we don't "air the misses," assuming we edit out the missed shots. Truth is, I can't afford to miss. I have aired a couple misses over the years, but honestly, with a good gun, quality scope and a steady shooting platform, I don't take a shot unless I'm almost certain I can make a clean kill.

How important is quality gear, from the gun to accessories and even my clothing? Of the last 97 big game animals I'd shot at with a rifle, 94 died. Again, I can't afford to miss, can't stand it when I do, so do all within my power to avoid letting it happen. Thankfully, once again, it all came together on this fine hunt.

Chapter 5:

Rimrock Muley

Idaho is known for holding big mule deer in certain areas. The Joseph Plains is one of those places.

I'd hunted with the fine staff at Boulder Creek Outfitters on several occasions, but never for mule deer. On previous hunts I had taken some dandy whitetails with them, along with elk, turkey and black bear, so when they invited me to hunt mule deer with them, I didn't hesitate accepting the offer.

Our goal was to film a TV show for Trijicon's Game Chasers, on the Outdoor Channel. I'd already taken a nice bull elk on the hunt, and with a few days remaining, our focus shifted to mule deer.

We wanted something big, or nothing. For this we concentrated our hunting efforts on the east side of the Joseph Plains, along the Salmon River Breaks, as well as along the western side of the Plains, along the Snake River Breaks. This country is big and brutally rugged, but holds big bucks.

Going on 30 years Tim Craig has been outfitting in this area, and every year they either tag or get a crack at a 190-inch or better buck. That's what we were hoping for on this hunt.

It was mid-October and unseasonably cold conditions hammered us right out the gate. It snowed hard on day one, the first snow Tim recalled seeing in 26 years of hunting on opening day. High winds carrying bone-chilling temperatures cut down the deer movement, but we were seeing good bucks, which kept our level of optimism high.

The only drawback, I had only two days to hunt. Our elk hunt had taken longer than expected, and I had to be in California in three days to film a blacktail deer hunt. This is one of those times when a demanding fall filming schedule can test a person's nerves and sanity. What I wouldn't give for an extra October!

It would have been easy to bag this hunt, but instead, we stayed positive and set out to accomplish the task at hand. Aaron Hensen, one of Boulder Creek's finest, would be the guide.

Heading into rugged rimrock country on the east side of the Joseph Plains, the terrain made the elk hills we'd been hunting appear gentle. Steep, rocky cliffs towering thousands of feet above the Salmon River made a hunter want to shoot nothing unless it was on the uphill side of a logging road.

Deer were plentiful from first-light through mid-day. Though we didn't see any shooters, we did see a handful of nice bucks in the 140 to 150-inch range. Following a short snack break, that afternoon we were back at it. It was cold, but calm. The first place we got out to glass, we found elk and deer, but no muleys that were big enough to move on.

Driving the quad around the hillside, Travis Ralls, my camera man, spotted a good buck. Travis was raised in central Oregon and has some of the best eyes of anyone I've hunted with. He's also the hardest working camera man I've ever had in the field. We put a move on the 170-inch class buck, but a pod of does got between us and botched the stalk before we could get any good footage of him.

Aaron Hensen with a shed antler he found high atop the Salmon River Breaks in Idaho. This is big, dangerous country, and Aaron knows it well.

The next and final morning of the hunt, we headed to a different place, on the west side of the plateau, into the unforgiving Snake River Breaks. Setting up to glass from a high, bald knob, a 140-inch 4x4 walked right by us at 30 yards. Aaron felt we could do better, so we let him be.

From that vantage point we glassed more than 20 does and a handful of average bucks. Then Aaron spotted some does well over a mile away. A buck was with them. It was so far, it was impossible to tell how big the buck was through binoculars, so we erected the spotting scope.

A closer look revealed a heavy-racked 4x4. "He's feeding up that hillside and will probably bed on the back side of it," Aaron noted. "If we hurry we might be able to catch him before he lays down."

We hustled, but when we poked our eyes over the rimrock, all we could see were does. Confident the

For 90 minutes, guide Aaron Hensen and I glassed from this spot for the buck we'd put a stalk on. Little did we know he was bedded 40 yards behind us the entire time.

buck hadn't left the ravine, we scoured every inch of land over the next 90 minutes. After seeing nothing, we resorted to trying to spook the buck out of there. We pushed out every doe, but no sign of the buck.

Dejected, we began our long hike back up the ridge from where we'd first spotted the buck. About halfway up we paused to catch our breath. That's when a vague, gray throat patch caught our eye. Closer inspection revealed just what we'd been looking for...our buck.

He was bedded tight to a patch of low-growing willows, not 40 yards from where we'd spent the last hour-and-a-half glassing for him. He'd circled back around beneath us, and given the steep hillside and height of the brush, we simply couldn't see him. He was there the entire time, literally close enough to hit with a rock. It was a classic mule deer maneuver that almost got us. Now came the hard part of stalking to within shooting range.

Detailing the route of our stalk, confidence levels ran high now that we had a second chance. There was no way the buck could escape without being seen, though given the brushy terrain, getting a shot was far from a sure bet.

We tiptoed across the top of our third and final ridge, which put us within 100 yards of where we last saw the buck. Nearly an hour had elapsed, but we were confident the buck was still there. Though we could see the exact brush he was bedded beneath, we failed to see a single hair of the deer. He was tucked in tight, and now it became a waiting game.

My most memorable mule deer stalk ever, this buck nearly gave us the slip. Big bucks like this are smart, and know how to use the terrain to their advantage.

Getting comfortable in the shooting sticks, I was prepared to spend however long it took for the buck to stand and show himself. It was a good six hours until he'd start feeding, so I really was hoping something would encourage him to get up before that time.

Then the wind changed. As it drifted across the draw and down toward the buck, he instantly stood and bolted. I had no shot but in desperation let out a loud grunt, hoping to stop him. It worked. At the top of a little granite finger – the final spot where it would even be possible to take a shot – the buck paused.

I was on him in an instant and wasted no time firing. Then I looked back at Travis, fearing what I thought to be the inevitable. Never was I so happy to see his smiling face, followed by the words, "I got it!"

The whole event unfolded so quickly, I was almost certain there wasn't enough time for Travis to catch it on film. How he picked up the buck in the camera, tracked him through the brush then held steady on the shot, was beyond me, but he pulled it off. In all honesty, it was one of the most memorable moments of my hunting career, for we'd just captured a big mule deer on film, in one of the most classic mule deer style stalks of my life.

At 106 yards, my shot was easy, but the buck disappeared over the ledge. It took several minutes of searching, but we found him, piled up in the middle of a thorn bush patch, 300 yards below where I'd hit him.

I was amazed to find he didn't break off any tines on his tumble down the near vertical, rocky hillside. Had he dropped on the spot, the pack out would have been easy. As it was, where he fell meant we'd have to bone him out and pack it all out on our backs. It added six hours to the finish work, but we didn't mind the extra pain, for the buck was everything I'd hoped for.

Though the old, heavy-racked brute fell well shy of the 190-inch mark we'd hoped for, none of us cared. I felt blessed to simply fill a tag on a short hunt like this. Such success speaks wonders for the guides, outfitter and hunting property.

In fact, of all the places I've been fortunate to hunt around the world, this is one of my favorites. The stunning scenery and breathtaking vantage points allow hunters to take in all this unique destination has to offer. Hunting in the same land as one of the most noted Native American tribes on the continent did, the Nez Perce, made this experience that much more special. How these fine hunters survived in such a rugged, unforgiving land centuries ago, is beyond me.

This is a place I hope to keep returning to, not only for the great animals that live here, but to rekindle the friendships I've developed. In the not so distant future, I hope my sons will be carrying their own rifles into these woods, experiencing the thrill of hunting this magical land as I've come to know it. All I ask is to be a small part of it, so I can continue living the dream.

Chapter 6:

Fence Post Whitetail

Known more for its mule deer than whitetails, Montana is one state that has whopper bucks of both species.

Walking through 10-inches of crusted snow, I made it into the tree stand an hour before sunup. The 12 below zero temperatures were balmy compared to the previous day, when I about froze in the stand at -22°. With a rise in temperature, it didn't take long to spot the first buck, a whitetail, moving along a grove of Russian olives.

He'd walk, make a scrape, lick a branch, move a few yards and do it all over again. He wasn't a big buck, no more than 120-inches in the rack. But he provided a level of optimism that gave me a gut feeling that it was going to be a good day.

The night before I watched a 150-inch buck from this same stand. He was a different 150 class buck than the one I'd seen only minutes prior, neither of which presented a shot. But sitting in that stand gave me the confidence to know I'd fill my tag. It was just a matter of time.

Over the course of the next two and half hours, I'd lay eyes on more than two dozen deer, several of which were bucks. Though none were the big bucks I'd seen the night before, I still had a good feeling about the day. As the morning wore on, curiosity got the best of me, and I couldn't help but hit the ground and inspect all the sign carving it's way through the freshly fallen snow. Walking was also a good excuse for me to try and warm my chilling body.

Tracks, well used trails and scrapes were everywhere. In my mind it was the big buck who laid the fresh scrape line in front of my stand, for it was along the same path I'd seen him partially emerge from the brush the night prior. Working my way into the bottom of a frozen-over slough, I felt certain I'd find the big buck, but good fortune was not with me.

Retracing my steps, I began working back toward the tree stand, headed for prime real estate 200 yards beyond it. This is where the brush-lined Yellowstone River meanders, a habitat known to hold big whitetail bucks. Approaching the stand I'd vacated 30 minutes earlier, the horizontal outline of a deer's back emanated from the tall, brown grass.

All alone, the deer fed along a beet field. Had I practiced patience and remained in the stand like I knew I should have, the 25 yard shot would have been simple. Now, 100 yards from where I crouched, his head was buried in grass, but there was little question the animal was a buck. His hefty body and wide back left no doubt he was a mature animal, but just how big was he?

With my shooting sticks buried in the snow, scope cranked to full power, I waited for the buck to lift his head. Closer he fed, until, finally at 80 yards he slowly brought his headgear above the grassline for the first time.

The right side of his rack was wide, but that was all I could see. "No way could the left antler be behind that fence post, that's too wide of a spread for him to carry," I pondered to myself. Praying the slight breeze wouldn't shift directions, I looked hard to find the other side of his rack. Unable to decipher what I so yearned to see, I could only surmise that he'd broken it off at the main beam, perhaps in a recent fight.

The buck sensed all was not right, and held firm for two minutes, not so much as even turning his head a fraction of an inch. With the crosshairs on his brisket, I wanted to pull the trigger in the worst way, but dared not to until I could see a matching antler on the other side of his head. From my position, a fat fence post still blocked the view.

It was the last week in November, and I was hunting with Shane Weiler, a man who has since become a dear friend. Hunting very near the town of Forsyth, Montana, Shane grew up in the region, and knows the people and the deer as well as anyone. With access to thousands of acres of prime whitetail and mule deer property, Shane is well aware of the gold mine on which he sits.

Shane and I were introduced by mutual friend, Chuck Johnson, the man who published my book, *A Flyfisher's Guide To Alaska*. Chuck knew Shane and I shared many of the same passions, and made it a point to make sure our paths crossed. The next thing I knew, I was hunting whitetails in Montana for the first time.

"The great thing about these whitetails is, no matter what tree stand you sit in, you'll see deer, and usually some good bucks," Shane told me as I crawled into my stand on the first evening of the hunt. Truth be told, I initially headed to Montana to try my luck on a big mule deer, but having been bitten by the western whitetail bug a few weeks prior, while hunting in Saskatchewan, I left my options open.

On day one of my Montana hunt, we sized-up mule deer in the morning, switching to whitetails in the afternoon. After seeing two whitetail bucks that would surpass my prized Saskatchewan gem, the decision was easy. It would be whitetails or nothing on this hunt.

"The last couple of years, antler growth hasn't been up to its full potential, due to dry conditions, though we did get a pretty nice 171-inch buck two years ago," noted Shane. "But last spring was a wet one, and antler growth improved."

By late November the rut was all but over and the bucks were concentrating on amassing fat for the brutal winter ahead. "We'll see a few bucks searching for does in the second rut now, but for the most part, the bigger bucks are going to be alone, feeding along brush lines," offered Shane. Right he was. What rutting activity and sign we did see, were the result of mostly smaller bucks.

Having sat in the stands, I was amazed at the number of deer I saw. Given the small home range of the whitetails living along the river bottom, being elevated in a tree stand means you're going to see more deer, especially as they move through thick brush and tall grass. But the buck I now faced was on the ground.

With the deer in my scope, still he hadn't moved. Finally, he took a few steps my way. Unfortunately, the wooden fence post continued to block my view of his left antler. Then he put his head down and went back to feeding. Nose back up, he snapped his head 90° and looked past the tree stand. For the first time I could see the buck carried a full rack, but due to the severe angle, I just couldn't tell how big it was.

In one fluid motion the buck took a couple steps and sailed over the fence, then bounded to my right. He had no idea I was there. Side-on, trotting as he was, I still failed to see what the left side of his rack looked like. My finger felt heavy on the trigger, and had I been able to confirm a matching antler, would have taken the shot. But I wanted to make sure.

Feeling an opportunity slipping away, I had no choice but to grunt with my voice. The buck stopped, alert and immediately zeroed in on my position. For the first time I saw his entire rack, and felt a surge of adrenaline shoot through my body as his antlers were even wider than I'd imagined.

Having been caught in a kneeling position when the buck moved from left to right, it tied up my legs. Daring not to readjust and risk spooking him, I knew the recoil of the .300 Remington Ultra Mag' would bury the scope between my eyes. For this buck, it was worth it.

At 80 yards a steady hold left no question that it was time to pull the trigger. I failed to see the impact of the bullet during recoil, due to my body's awkward position. Twirling in the snow to readjust my legs, as the deer sprinted off I lost sight of him when he darted behind a mass of fallen trees. Then I could feel it. Blood flowed down my nose, pocking the ivory snow at my feet. The scope had, indeed, smacked me between the eyes.

This is still my biggest Montana whitetail. Given the fact the left side of his rack remained hidden behind a fence post for so long, I couldn't decide if he was a buck worth pulling the trigger on or not. Then he stepped into the clear.

Rounding out this memorable hunt, Shane Weiler and I took in a Thanksgiving morning goose hunt.

Eager to see the results of the shot, I applied pressure with my gloved hand to the cut between my eyes, then quickly picked up the buck's tracks. Blood-stained snow was everywhere, confirming a good, double-lung hit. Following the tracks around the fallen trees, I just had to laugh to myself when I found the buck dead, less than 10-feet from the tree stand in which I had sat.

The buck wasn't the biggest in the river bottom, in fact, three other bucks were definitely larger than this one. But in Montana, when a 5x6 buck with impressive eye-guards and a 22-inch spread stands broadside to me, I'm taking him.

After caping the buck and taking care of the meat, Shane and I spent the next three days together experiencing some of eastern Montana's great wing-shooting. Taking sharptail grouse, pheasants and a Merriam's turkey offered more great food for the pot.

On my final day, Thanksgiving, Shane and I set out an impressive spread of Canada goose decoys. It was only a matter of minutes before we secured our limits of those, too. Hopping out of the blind, walking across the field to retrieve my final honker, I could look up and see the tree stand in which I sat for deer.

Heading back to the blind, honkers continued pouring in to the decoys. Shane and I just sat, taking in the magical moment. Though my Montana smorgasbord hunting adventure was drawing to a close, I knew I'd be back one day, hunting with Shane Weiler.

Today, Shane and I are close friends, and we've shared many great hunts together. He's the kind of man I see myself hunting with for the rest of my life, and one day, I bet our children will be doing the same. It's friendships like this that make hunting so special.

Chapter 7:

Moose On Horseback

Some hunts never go quite as planned. On this journey, our plans changed, but in the end everything came together.

Of all North America's big game animals, nothing shocks a hunter more than walking up on a downed moose. The task of caping, field dressing and boning out a giant bull moose seems like an overwhelming task that's nearly impossible to tackle with a simple knife.

Over the past 20 years, the popularity of moose hunting has grown considerably. Be it the monster Alaska-Yukon moose, the Shiras or Canadian moose, more and more hunters are yearning to hunt these grand animals, the largest member of our deer family.

British Columbia's Tuchodi River Valley is one of the most stunning places I've set foot in. It served as the perfect backdrop for this horseback moose hunting adventure.

This hunt found me once again with Larry and Lori Warren, of Tuchodi River Outfitters. Our target was the Canadian moose subspecies. I'd taken Alaska-Yukon moose while living in Alaska, but had never hunted the Canadian moose, until now. Situated in the Tuchodi River Valley, in northern British Columbia, the Warren's have access to more land than they can possibly hunt. At the time of my hunt, their concession encompassed 3,500 square miles, over four million acres.

Pouring over the many maps of their hunting area, and seeing how massive that much land truly takes in, I wasn't surprised when Larry told me they don't even get to hunt a third of the land due to its remote, rugged nature. There are also so many animals in this region, there's not often a need to explore beyond the lands already conquered.

This was to be a classic horseback hunt, what Tuchodi River Outfitters is known for. Our goal was to try for a record-class bull with antlers spanning in the middle to upper 50-inch range. Originally, Larry, himself, was to serve as the guide on this hunt, but a sudden change of plans botched that.

The day before we were to leave base camp and ride the 20-some miles on horseback, one of the Warren's clients fell off a horse and suffered severe injuries. A broken hip, pelvis and back left the hunter in agony. The worst part, bad weather prevented search and rescue aircrafts from reaching him for two days.

When the accident happened, my moose hunting plans changed. Understandably, Larry had to stick close to camp. The injured hunter was in good hands with professional guides, wranglers and other hunters in his party, but they were over 40 miles from base camp, at one of Tuchodi's spike camps.

Now the plans were for me to hunt moose from base camp. This isn't something they normally do, but given the severe circumstances, to be honest, I was just happy I still had the opportunity to go on the hunt. It could have easily been postponed, indefinitely, with good reason.

The Warren's run some 150 head of horses, year-round, in the Tuchodi River Valley. At the start of each season, wranglers scour the valleys and hills rounding up horses. At the end of each season, the horses are cut loose to fend for themselves. They overwinter surprisingly well, and quickly settle down for easy riding once wrangled.

Early the next morning, after gathering some horses, my young guide, Josh Johnson, assured me we'd see moose. Josh had recently ridden through the valley we intended on hunting and saw some good bulls on his way to a Stone sheep hunt. That was the kind of information I loved hearing, for it greatly boosted my confidence.

Granted, the size of the bull we now sought dropped, considering we were only hunting five miles from base camp, but Josh still thought we might be able to break the prized 50-inch mark. At this point, given the situation in the camp, I would have been happy with any legal bull.

I love trying for trophy class animals, but when the situation doesn't feel right, I won't push it. What happens, happens, and all we could ask for at this point was an opportunity at a good representative bull. That's all I wanted.

On our awe-inspiring ride up the drainage which fed into the Tuchodi River Valley, I was surprised at how quickly we gained elevation. I was also glad we were on horseback, for from where we started along the banks of the river, we easily covered 2,000 feet in elevation on our initial ascent. When you're nearly looking Stone sheep eye-to-eye, you know you're up there.

It was one of the most enjoyable horseback rides I'd ever been on, other than the fact I was suffering from a torn disk in my lower back. Because of the back pain I was in, however, I was forced to dismount and walk every 20 minutes or so. When we hit the timber, I actually preferred walking over riding, thanks to the plentiful number of bull elk in the area.

Prior to heading out for moose, I took this elk. Never had I seen so many elk in one area, or called in so many bulls in one day.

Earlier on the hunt I'd taken a nice bull with my bow. Never had I seen so many elk in one place in all the years I've hunted them. A buddy and I called in over 20 bulls one day, and filled two tags, both with our bows.

While heading to our moose grounds, I couldn't help but make seductive cow elk calls when walking through the timber. More than a dozen bulls responded to the calls, and a few even came in, bugling virtually every step of the way. Bugling elk are something I never tire of, even if my tag has already been filled.

Tuchodi River Outfitters is known for producing outstanding Stone sheep, as this hunter confirms.

Breaking out above the timberline, the scenery was stunning. The commanding view we had of the Tuchodi Valley and its surrounding hills made me want to simply slow down time. The weather was perfect, not to hot, not too cold. The golden leaves had begun to drop with regularity from the vast aspen groves and the smell of fall was in the air. It was one of those days that makes me especially proud to be a hunter, for were it not for our sport, I would not be feasting my eyes on some of the most striking country God's created.

At one point, where we stopped to rest the horses, Josh pointed to where a wolf had recently been taken. He also showed me some of the better Stone sheep peaks in the area. The Stone sheep is one of those animals I'll likely not get an opportunity to hunt in my lifetime, simply due to the lofty price tag attached to them. I'm fine with that, but forever remain optimistic, for I never thought I'd have the good fortune of partaking in many of the hunts that I have over the past few years. I have TV to thank for that, without a doubt.

Josh also pointed up one big drainage, showing where some nice grizzlies had been taken over the years. The outfitter isn't alloted many grizzly tags, but the ones they do get usually are filled on big, mature boars.

Hopping back in the saddle, we started making our way deeper into the valley. I was amazed at how much it opened up, exposing prime moose habitat, the likes of which I had no idea existed so near to base camp.

"We usually start seeing moose right down in this bowl," Josh whispered as we tied off the horses to the only tree around. Crawling up to the crest of the ridge, we peeked over the edge, into the little valley.

Though tags are limited, Tuchodi River Outfitters kicks-out some giant grizzlies for their clients.

First a cow, then another, then a third. "There's got to be a bull in here with this many cows," Josh urged. It was late September and the moose rut was in full-swing. Three more cows appeared, then a bull finally popped into view. Breaking out the spotting scope, Josh confirmed that he was a legal bull.

He was still a good half-mile away, and though he was legal, we weren't yet sure if he was the bull we wanted. No question he was in a good location, and given the wind direction, we agreed he was worth taking a closer look at. It was still early enough in the day that I could be a little picky on the size of bull we were after.

Skirting around the back side of the ridge we were on, we cut the 800 yard distance to 300. By that time, a couple cows were starting to feed away from us and the bull was following. Short tundra separated us from the group, and rather than risk being seen in an attempt to get closer, Josh made a perfect sounding moose call with his voice.

Immediately the bull looked our way, sniffed the air and answered back. The sight of his massive rack being tossed across his back, his bells flapping and massive snout turning to the sky is an image I'll not soon forget. Grabbing a big, white limb, Josh held it horizontally above his head and let out another call. The flashing white limb – meant to mimic another bull's rack – caught our bull's attention. Again he bellowed back at us, then started coming.

By now we'd had a good look at every angle of the bull's rack. He wasn't the biggest moose on the block, but he was plenty good for me. "He won't go 50-inches, but he has good tine length and pretty fair width on his upper palms," confirmed Josh. "It's your call."

My decision had already been made. We were filming this hunt for an episode of Trijicon's Game Chasers and everything was coming together nicely. This is one of those situations where, when things are right for TV, you roll with it no matter how bad a record book animal may be desired. Fact was, we had a good moose within range, he was cooperating perfectly for the camera and he was in a prime location for getting the pack horses in.

Given the rugged valley that separated us from the bull, we didn't want him to come any closer, for fear of not being able to get a shot due to the severe, steep angle of the terrain. The decision was made to shoot across the little draw.

While Travis situated the camera and tripod for the shot, I ranged the bull. Just over 270 yards. Given the size of a bull moose, even at that distance Travis confirmed he'd look great on TV. One thing we try to achieve when filming shows is to get close, intimate shots of animals so viewers can connect with them. This allows the audience to feel more of the excitement of the hunt. Many times

Given the situation, I couldn't have been more pleased with the outcome of my one day Canada moose hunt.

we won't take the shot if this element is missing.

With the range nailed down, and Travis secure on the tripod, all we needed now was for the bull to turn broadside. He'd walked back into a grove of spruce trees, but a few calls from Josh brought the bull back into the open.

As the bull slowly walked into an opening on the opposite hillside, I nestled the .300 Winchester Magnum into my pack for a secure rest. When the moose presented his left side, I squeezed the trigger. The 180 grain bullet pierced both lungs, and sent the bull running.

A fitting end to a perfect hunt. This is a place I hope to one day return to.

Fearing he'd sprint downhill, making for a longer pack job, I hit the bull one more time. That shot dropped him.

Walking up to our bull, I was amazed by his body size, just as I always am when approaching a downed moose. After snapping some photos, Josh hiked back up the hill and led the horses to within a few hundred yards of the kill. In the meantime, Travis and I skinned and quartered the moose. The next day was spent with a string of pack horses, hauling the moose out of the valley.

My dreams of hunting Canadian moose had been realized. The bull's rack carried 21 points and fell a bit shy of 50-inches. The fact this caliber of bull was taken only four hours from base camp made me more than happy. We'd completed the task of attaining a good TV show, and that was our number one priority.

As for the hunter who had fallen off his horse, it took two days, but he finally made it to medical attention. He spent several days in the hospital, but the last I heard, was recovering nicely, thank goodness.

On wilderness horseback hunts, you never know what will happen. There are always risks, but without taking these risks, hunters will never get to enjoy the sheer beauty such excursions have to offer.

Chapter 8:

Double Drop Twine Muley

Getting any deer with a drop tine is special, but when that buck is a mule deer with double drop tines, the game intensifies.

"There's a really neat buck I just saw while driving home tonight," shared Shanna Howell. "He's not very wide, but he has drop tines on each side."

The moment I hung up the phone, I knew this was the buck I'd be dreaming about for the next four months, even though I'd never laid eyes on him.

A lot could happen from the time Shanna first saw the buck in July, and the time I'd be hunting with her and her husband Guy, owners of Center of the Nation Outfitters, in the far northeast corner of Wyoming, in November. Over the course of the next couple months the Howells would see the buck, but once he shed his velvet, his movements became secretive.

Once the buck started moving at night, the sightings became less frequent, to the point the Howell's thought that perhaps the buck had left their vast acreage. Then, in late September they spotted him again, on their land.

In the middle of October, 2006, I'd get the opportunity to meet the Howells for the first time. It was a pronghorn hunt which took me there, and though speedgoats were the target this time around, it was the double drop tine muley that I really yearned to catch a glimpse of. Fortunately, I'd see the grand buck, twice.

The first time I saw the double drop tine buck was in the headlights. We were traveling the country road into Howell's property, and a nice mule deer crossed in front of us. He stopped along the edge of the road and we turned the headlights on him. There stood the buck, complete with two drop tines. He looked big, but just how big was hard to accurately assess in the less than ideal lighting conditions.

The next morning found us headed into the pronghorn flats. Driving across the ranch we saw plenty of pronghorns, several whitetails, and a lone muley buck bedded on the sunny side of a timbered knoll. "He looks like a good buck, you might want to try and go snap a photo of him," smiled Guy. I was focused on pronghorns and didn't really get excited, but Guy kept urging me to step out and take a look.

The moment I put the glass to my eyes, my heart raced. There he was, less than 150 yards away, the double drop tine buck. He looked far superior in daylight than in darkness. The sun bounced off his gor-

Guy Howell has some 40,000 acres in the extreme northeast corner of Montana. Over the course of several hunts with him, we've covered it all.

geous pelage, highlighting his distinct rack and striking double throat patch. It was obvious he wasn't an old deer. Then again, it was clear that any hunter who saw him wouldn't let him live another year.

His perfect 4x4 rack sported nice eye-guards and two matching drop tines. Gravity seemed to pull the drop tines from the main frame, stretching them at least five inches toward the ground. There's no question he was the same buck I'd seen the night prior, in the headlights. But this time he looked magnificent.

"He's been staying in the area pretty regularly the past couple of weeks," pointed out Guy. "But he is right on the property line, and I know the neighbors have their eyes on him." Had the buck been in the center of Howell's land, I'd have lost fewer hairs over the next 18 days, the time my deer hunt was to take place with Guy.

After a successful pronghorn hunt with Guy, I'd return in early November, praying the drop tine buck was still alive. By the time I arrived for the deer hunt, the season had been open for a few days. All I could do was keep my fingers crossed that the buck stayed on Howell's property, and that no other hunters had taken him.

Raised on a ranch, seeing Guy Howell on a horse, whether he's working or hunting, is an every day routine.

Upon my arrival, the first question I asked was, "Is the double drop tine buck still alive?" Guy smiled. There was no need for words, I knew the answer.

"But something's happened, and I think it's helped keep him alive," Guy smirked. "He got the left side of his rack tangled in some orange bailing twine, and you can't make out what that side of his rack is like."

Howell pointed out that the buck had got into the twine a few days after my antelope hunt. He was worried that it would stress the deer, and that he'd go into hiding in the back country. Though the buck did go into hiding the first few days, Guy was seeing him from time to time, not far from where we watched him that glorious morning of my pronghorn hunt. He still teetered on the edge of the property line, but he was still alive.

The next morning couldn't come fast enough. The first place we settled in to glass from, all we saw were a couple whitetails. "The last time I saw him, he was over on that ridge, just below the big timber," pointed Guy. We glassed the area, but saw nothing.

The thing that made me nervous was the fact that where the buck was last seen, was no more than a few hundred yards from the property line. When we failed to find him, I grew even more anxious.

Then we relocated. Guy found a big whitetail buck first, and though he was worth a closer look, I couldn't get excited about him. My heart was set on finding that drop tine buck. I watched a whitetail doe as she fed through a meadow, behind a patch of brush. As she disappeared, the hind end of a mule deer caught my eye. Stepping to the side, a shot of adrenaline coursed through my body as the next thing I saw was a ball of orange twine.

No question, this was our buck, but he was over a half-mile away, in the open. We had no choice but to watch, and see where the buck went. As morning progressed, the buck moved from the grassy meadow and melted into a wooded ridge, still on Guy's property.

"Perfect!" exclaimed Guy. "He's going to get on the south side of the ridge and bed there for the day. Let's get moving."

We scampered up the ridge, trying to catch a glimpse of the buck. Temperatures that morning were cold, into single-digits, and the ground was noisy. This meant our going was slower than we would have liked, but we had no choice. One wrong move could blow it. The last thing we wanted to do was push him across the property line.

When we finally did get to the funnel we thought the buck moved into, he was nowhere to be seen. Our slow progress allowed the buck to move out well ahead of us. Now we had to start all over again.

"He must have moved higher up the ridge," whispered Guy. Within 200 yards the ridgeline began to flatten out, and the timber grew sparse. We saw some muley does feeding, but no sign of the buck, or any buck for that matter. Given the time of year, the rut could kick-in at any moment, and the sighting of does in the area instilled needed confidence.

We continued stealthing our way through the open timber, searching for the buck. We'd walk, stop and glass. Then, across the farthest opening, we spotted our deer, nibbling on some grass. Does were near, but he showed no interest in them. His neck was far from swollen, and the fact he fed so intently signaled that breeding was not foremost on his mind.

"You're on your own from here," offered Guy.

Guy stayed back, keeping an eye on the buck as I slithered from pine tree to pine tree. Though the trees thinned out the closer I got to the deer, they were still large enough and staggered perfectly, serving as ideal cover. At 160 yards, I had a clear shot, but right then the buck moved behind a pile of brush.

I grew nervous, for the towering pile of slash that lay on the side of a hill provided him with cover. Should the buck choose to work his way downhill, on the back side of the slash pile, I might never see him again. If I tried moving forward to cut him off and he did step out, I'd be busted, for there were

With one side of his rack covered in bailing twine, I wasn't sure this buck still carried his matching drop tine that was seen on him a couple weeks earlier.

no more trees between the two of us.

Slowly I spread the legs of the shooting sticks, and carefully placed them in front of and to the right side of the last tree. Seconds later the buck stepped out from behind the brush pile.

As I settled the Thompson Center ProHunter, chambered in .300 Winchester Magnum, into position and put the point of the Trijicon AccuPoint scope square on his right shoulder, time stood still. The buck was contentedly feeding, comfortable in his familiar setting. All the anticipation of the past few months had come down to this one moment.

In a way, I wasn't ready for it to end. I took in every precious second of observation as the buck moved, unaware of my presence. He was one of the most beautiful mule deer I'd ever laid eyes on.

Then, he sensed something wasn't right. The buck quickly lifted his head, stiffened his ears and used his nose to sniff the air. I knew the time was now.

Pulling the hammer back, I slowly applied pressure on the trigger. The roar of the rifle surprised me as it sent a 180-grain Remington Swift Scirocco bullet his way. Simultaneously, steam rolled from the entrance and exit wounds of the buck, as well as from his mouth. It was a reminder of just how cold and crisp this early morning was. In classic action, the buck's hind end dropped first, and he tipped completely backwards.

Admittedly, even though the buck was dead, I was still a bit curious, almost nervous. For though I could clearly see the big ball of twine on the left side of the buck's rack, the biggest question in my mind was whether or not all his tines were still intact.

I distinctly recall seeing – as soon as the buck threw his head up – something dangling from the orange twine. At that distance I couldn't tell if it was a branch or a broken tine. Approaching the downed buck, I was about to find out.

Lifting the rack of the buck, I was relieved to see that it was, indeed, a stick that had become entangled in the twine. It was about the same thickness of it's tines, which is what threw me.

Cutting the twine from the buck's rack, I was relieved to see a perfect drop tine, six-inches in length, a mirror image to the one on the opposite side. Stepping back, taking a look at

With the bailing twine removed, I was elated to find a truly unique set of perfect antlers. Not only was this buck's rack eye-catching, but he had one of the most beautiful capes of any mule deer I'd taken.

the elegant buck, not only did his captivating rack demand my attention, but his striking cape was among the most magnificent I'd seen on any mule deer.

Though he wasn't the biggest, oldest mule deer I'd taken by any means, he was a very special buck. The fact my obsession for him began with a friendly phone conversation four months prior, and ended in a tangled mess of twine, made it all the more special.

Today, when I look up from my office desk, the one I'm writing this book from, the first mounted animal I see is that double drop tine buck. It's funny, for what I see now differs greatly from how he looked through the scope in those final few moments of the hunt. But I can still close my eyes and see that glowing ball of orange twine tangled on the left side of his rack, wondering if there was a hidden drop tine in there. Then I open my eyes and just smile.

Chapter 9:

South Dakota Speedgoat

Big Pronghorns can pop-up just about anywhere, but the results of this hunt even surprised me.

Being born and raised in Oregon, I've held a deep passion for the array of big game species that live here. I've hunted most of them, excluding, of course, big horn sheep and mountain goat, the two toughest tags to draw. I've also had terrible luck when it comes to drawing an antelope tag. In fact, up to now, I've still never hunted pronghorns in my home state.

Out of frustration, and a burning desire to experience what pronghorn hunting is all about, I started venturing out of state. Today, I've been fortunate to take several antelope in multiple states, with both rifle and bow. One thing I've learned, these animals are addicting to hunt.

Pronghorn, antelope, speedgoats, goats...whatever you want to call them, they're a true joy to hunt, especially for a kid who grew up chasing blacktails in the dense forests of western Oregon. Being able to see for miles, and watch hundreds of animals on a single hunt, usually in nice, warm weather, makes pronghorns a truly unique pleasure to hunt.

Prior to this hunt, my best pronghorn bucks had come from Montana and Wyoming. None were record-breaking bucks, but several were big enough to qualify for the books. Over the past few years I'd hunted pronghorns with my bow in South Dakota, too. Though I didn't take any monsters, my eyes were opened when good friend, Reese Clarkson, took me to another section of land.

I've been hunting with Clarkson, owner of Mill Iron Outfitters, for years. We've filmed several television shows together and I can honestly say Reese is one of my favorite people on this planet. You won't meet a more morally upstanding, hard working, kinder man. His family is also charming, as are his father, Bill, the sheriff for Harding County, and his mother, Shirley, one of the kindest women I've met – her cooking talents also rival those of my wife's! I love being around these people so much, one spring I loaded my family in the truck and drove out to spend time with Reese and his family.

Early one fall, while driving between deer hunting spots, Reese took a detour to show me a chunk of ground he would soon have access to. "It doesn't have any muleys on it," he pointed out, "but it has some good goats. I'm thinking of running some rifle hunts on it next year."

When I saw the magnitude of pronghorn bucks on this piece of land, I told Reese to put me down for next season, should I be fortunate enough to draw a tag. The odds of drawing a rifle tag for a nonresident in this part of northwestern South Dakota weren't great, but they were better than what I'd been getting in Oregon.

The next summer I was elated to draw the tag, and Reese and I made plans to hunt together in early October. First light found us parked on a sidehill, overlooking vast meadows of golden grass and sage brush flats. In the distance, rocky spires jutted from the desert floor, catching the first hint of sunlight.

"There's been a nice goat hanging around here," whispered Reese. "He'll go 17-inches, should score real well given his mass and cutter length."

I've been fortunate to hunt many times with Reese Clarkson, and will never tire of the experience. He's one of the finest men I've ever met.

Within 100 yards of where we sat glassing, a dandy buck with horns over 15-inches fed into view, joined by two other lesser bucks. He was tall, very symmetrical and one of the most striking bucks I'd ever seen. Had it not been in the opening minutes of our hunt, I would have been more than happy to put my tag on him. "Don't even think about it," smirked Reese. "There's bigger goats than that out here. Let's try and find that big boy, first."

Within two hours we glassed over 15 bucks, one of which was a shooter. He wasn't the 17-incher, but he was definitely pushing 16-inches, with good ivory tips.

He was with a group of does, and though the rut had passed, he stuck tight to them, smack in the middle of a wide-open meadow. The closest we could get was 400 yards. The nearer we moved, the further out the speedgoats shifted, until they slithered under a livestock fence and found safety on a neighboring property.

This was one of those times where it was frustrating to have the TV cameras along. For everyone who has the misconception that filming hunts for television is easy, believe me, it's far from it. As if filling a tag when hunting alone isn't hard enough, throw in a guide, usually a buddy who is willing to help out and a camera man or two, and just like that the complexity of the hunt grows exponentially.

Try walking through the woods, or in this case the desert, with an entourage and barely enough cover to hide your boot laces. It sometimes amazes me that we put any animals down, let alone get 26 hunts a year on film. Unforeseen challenges are always looming, no doubt.

Then there's the fact that the animal has to be within camera range. Mind you, camera range is much different than gun range – this is especially true with low-power lenses. Unfortunately, we had a low-power lens on this hunt, as our #1 camera was being repaired.

Dealing with cacti is a common occurrence when hunting this part of the American West.

When filming out West, I like having cameras with at least a 16 power lens, preferably 20 power or more. A higher magnification lens allows long distance shots to be made, whereby letting us wrap up shows in a timely manner. It also allows us to make longer shots on animals without having to chance getting closer and risk spooking them.

On our pronghorn hunt with Reese, our backup camera had an 8 power lens, about the last choice you want when filming an open-country hunt like this. This meant we'd have to get within 200 yards of our target if we wanted viewers to be able to clearly recognize what we were shooting. This also explains why I wasn't able to take a shot at that first record book buck we saw – though he was within rifle range, the camera simply couldn't reach out to 400 yards. That buck lived because of TV.

We found another Booner buck a few minutes later, but were unable to get in shooting position before losing sight of him for good. As early evening approached, pronghorns began milling about. From every gully and sage brush-choked draw, the animals trickled into the nutrient-rich, grass fields to feed.

Seeing a tall, fairly wide but stunningly symmetrical buck, my heart pounded in anticipation. I knew then and there he was one I wanted. Clarkson encouraged me to take a closer look through the spotting scope. "I'll be darn, the same buck we saw at first light?" I quizzed. Clarkson nodded his head, "Yip."

Truth be told, I wanted that buck ever since laying eyes on him, and the fact we passed him right out the gate had me second-guessing myself the entire day. Now, it was time to make a move.

He was with two other bucks, and we watched as they walked over a brush-covered knoll, into an old wash. Figuring we could get above them, we wasted no time. Once we got there, the little gully was filled with pronghorns feeding, bedding and seeking relief from the wind.

Then a doe saw us, grew nervous and the herd of more than 50 animals split in every direction. It was hard telling which buck was ours. We thought we had him pegged, made a stalk, then discovered it was the wrong buck. Then Clarkson found him, nearly a mile away, feeding in a short grass field.

Using sparse trees and undulating terrain as cover, we meandered our way into shooting position. At just over 300 yards, the buck fed, totally unaware of our presence. We watched as the buck continued feeding. Fortunately, he was moving our way.

We really wanted that buck to get within 200 yards before taking the shot, but we were up against time. At 275 yards I asked my camera man, Bret Stuart, if I could shoot. He shot me a look as if to say, "You know better than to ask me that!" Bret was one of the best off-hand camera men I've ever worked with, and he was raised hunting and fishing. He knows his stuff, including what it takes to make good TV shows.

"Let him get a little closer," Bret encouraged. He knew the sun was setting and that our optimal filming light would soon be lost.

The two pronghorns that our target buck fed behind, turned and started working up a hillside, broadside to our position. "Take him any time," Bret whispered, knowing the buck wasn't going to get any closer. The range was just beyond 250 yards.

This was the third largest buck we saw on this pronghorn hunt, a true testimony to the caliber of bucks living in the northwest corner of South Dakota.

Taking a steady rest in the shooting sticks, I firmly settled the apex of the Trijicon scope high on the buck's shoulder. No sooner had the 6.8mm barked when a report came back of the bullet finding its mark. The buck ran a short distance and collapsed.

Approaching the fallen animal, there was no ground shrinkage on this one, something that commonly happens with pronghorns. His horns spanned a fraction shy of 16-inches, and though he barely missed making the Boone & Crockett record book, I didn't care. On that day, we saw three other bucks larger than the one I'd just shot, a testimony to what a sleeper spot this section of South Dakota is amid pronghorn hunting circles.

I've been fortunate to take several good pronghorns, and mule deer, with Reese Clarkson over the years, and always look forward to spending time in the field with him. In fact, it's Reese and his friendship that I covet most. I guess I have the state of Oregon to partially thank, for had I ever drawn a tag there, who knows if the paths of Reese and I would have ever crossed.

Chapter 10:

The Toughest Bear Of All

I love hunting bears, and have pursued them in many states, in a wide-range of conditions. From polar bears to grizzlies, brown bears to black bears, each and every bear hunting scenario is unique unto itself. Up to this point, I've taken more than two dozen black bears in my life, not a lot, but a fairly solid number. Of all the bear hunts I've been on, the two toughest took place behind a pack of hounds. This was one of them.

Echoing off canyon walls, the incessant bawls of the hound pack dissipated as they rounded a ridge in the seemingly endless, timbered valley below. Barking with every stride, they were no doubt on the heels of the bear they'd struck two hours prior. My hunting partner, Randy Collins, and I stood, listening, hoping the bear would pull himself out of the deep canyon before treeing.

No such luck.

In the steepest canyon he'd been through all morning, the bear treed amongst a stand of old growth Douglas firs. It took us over an hour to reach the pack, stuck to the base of the tree like children clinging to a new Christmas toy. Working for a clean shot on the bruin, the job intensified once he hit the ground. At 250-plus pounds, getting him out of the hole wasn't easy. There were no roads below, forcing us to battle brush and gravity on our uphill journey.

Four hours later we made it to an old skid road, beaten, wet and exhausted. I was a sophomore in college at the time, and it was my first bear hunting experience with hounds. Right there I vowed to never hunt black bears again with hounds in the rugged mountains of Oregon's Cascade Range.

In the rugged slopes of the western Cascades and Coast Range, bear hunting with hounds can be among the most physically demanding hunts in all North America.

A year later I was behind dogs once again, this time in quest of a cougar. At the time, this was a legal practice in my home state of Oregon, and I'd love nothing more than to see this very efficient means of hunting once again reinstated.

On this day, a fresh skiff of snow had fallen, making tracking ideal. But the cats weren't moving. Skirting the edge of an old apple orchard we came across bear tracks, big bear tracks. My buddy on this hunt, veteran houndsman Max Arms, wanted to turn his dogs loose in the worst way and given the size of the tracks, I couldn't blame him.

The wooded canyon we stood in was enormous, and I figured the bear would tree somewhere along its gentle fringes. Cutting the pack loose, they were on the bear in no time. Four hours later they were still going. My vows had been thrown to the wind.

Five hours into the chase we intercepted the hound pack along the last accessible logging road. By this time the hunt had gained a couple thousand feet in elevation, taking us higher into the unforgiving Cascade Mountains. The bear was a big boar, obviously one that had no intentions of seeking refuge in a tree any time soon. The worst part, he was heading into a deep, dark canyon which marked the beginning of a roadless wilderness area.

By this time, Harold, one of Max's longtime hunting partners had joined us, anxious to get his hounds working. Nabbing a few of Max's dogs that had run themselves ragged, we spiced up the pack with some fresh blood. Then the Collins brothers joined us, a hard-core pair who measured their bear hunting success in how far they traveled across rugged country, not how many bears they treed. I'd hunted with these brothers before, and knew what I was in for. It was only the beginning.

At one point we had 17 hounds on the bear, and though we could hear him bay up, he never would tree. With no logging roads from which to operate, it was now a foot race. Over fallen trees, through thick brush and up creeks, we struggled to stay within earshot of the hounds.

This hunt took place in the days before fancy radio tracking devices were found on every hound's collar. Hunters primarily tracked their dog packs by ear, and with no logging roads left to drive along, keeping up on foot was the only option. Considering the price tag on some of the bloodlines in the pack, we all worked hard to keep up. The average cost for each of these hounds was around $3,000, with some worth considerably more than that.

Running through dense brush found our bodies soaking wet, minutes after bailing off into the woods. One of the toughest tests came when we took a shortcut across a unit that had recently been logged. The fir trees were laying down and had been limbed, but not yarded. For over a quarter mile, through a driving rain, most of our running was done on logs. We hopped from log to log, sprinted as far as we could, then log-hopped again.

I took more terrible spills than I care to admit, getting buried in the labyrinth of limbs laying between the downed trees and the ground. Shins and arms bloody, my body was taking more of a pounding than from any football game I'd endured. The four men I hunted with were all loggers, and wore their calks (specially designed boots with steel spikes in them used for walking on logs). They easily found traction when treading on the logs. I, on the other hand, spent more time on my back than on my feet.

Once through the clearing, I was amazed to find I had no broken bones in my body. I was soaked to the skin, but warm given the amount of body heat I was generating on this intense hunt.

The chase led into a brushy canyon, the clearest point of which to travel through was smack up a roaring creek. Dense brush lined the creek on both sides, and there was no option other than running up the creek if we wanted to keep up with the pack.

When trailing packs of hounds like this, I quickly learned that the straightest line between two points is the only way. It didn't matter how rough the going got, the goal was to cover ground and keep track of the dogs.

Due to the roaring creek that was waist-deep in spots, we lost ear contact with the pack. Still, given the rout the bear was taking, we were sure he was continuing straight up the canyon.

Being around the thundering chaos of a treed bear is intense, and offers a whole new energy level that must be experienced to be fully appreciated.

Intense rain pelted us for hours as we struggled to keep our footing on logs, rocks and mud. With one more summit to clear before disappearing into a seemingly endless canyon, the dogs finally barked treed. Making our way to the giant tree wasn't easy, for we had to get there in a hurry, before the bear decided to hit the ground running.

When we did arrive at the base of the giant, old growth Douglas fir, the barking of the hounds was so intense, we couldn't hear one another talk. Worse yet, we could hardly see the bear. He sat more than 70 feet up in the massive tree, oversized limbs growing nearly to the ground. Getting a shot was not going to be easy.

Tying off the dogs on the uphill side of the big tree so they wouldn't get nailed by the falling bear when I shot him, we discovered many of them were covered in wounds. These are scars they'll carry for life, carved into them when battling this bayed bear as he fought off their aggressive attacks.

Finally, after several minutes of maneuvering around the tree, a tiny window presented itself. Steadying the 4X scope of the .30-06 on the bear's massive neck, I expected him to crumble at the shot. Instead, there was no reaction. A quick second shot to the spine smacked home, and as he turned to bite the entry wound, another shot to the neck sent him crashing through the trees. Falling like a freight train, I was stunned to see how easily the limbs busted off the huge tree as the bear plunged toward earth. Limbs the size of a grown man's leg, snapped like toothpicks under the hulking mass of the bear.

When the bruin hit the ground with a resounding thug, he was lifeless. The hounds howled in victory, and I could only think about our long walk out of this arduous land. Once dead, bears are not easy to deal with. All the fun of bear hunting stops the moment the trigger is pulled.

Utilizing a chain saw winch to drag the bear from the high country took hours. The men I'd hunted with had been working with hounds their entire lives. They wanted to get that bear on a scales, for it was the largest they'd ever taken. They committed to getting this bear out of the woods, whole.

The brute squared just over seven feet and tipped the scales to 407 pounds. His skull measured over 20-inches, an exceptional bear for the Cascade Range. For the state of Oregon he was a giant bear, the largest the houndsmen's group told me that had been recorded in the state in the past 17 years.

While skinning and butchering that bear, I got an infection in the many cuts my arms and hands suffered earlier in the day. That progressed into a dangerously high fever, then blood poisoning. Even after the hunt was over, the pain from the experience wasn't. Fortunately, I fully recovered.

Two weeks following the bear hunt we were back in the woods. I was with Harold, once again, and we only had two dogs along. This day found us searching for cougar, our initial target the day we killed the big bear. When the dogs barked strike, I winced, praying it wasn't another bear.

In less than 15 minutes we had a big tom perfectly perched in a big fir tree. The shot with a .22 magnum was easy, and the 155 pound, 6-foot 9-inch tom was down. The cougar was a notorious sheep killer, who, the night prior,

Following one of the most rigorous hunting days of my life, I ended up with this hefty Oregon bear. After getting cleaned up and drying out, the outcome was worth the pain and effort, but at the time of the chase I was feeling otherwise.

Two weeks after taking my biggest bear with hounds, I took this cougar by the same means. The chase on this cat lasted only minutes.

killed 12 head before finding one he could drag under a livestock fence to feast on. Given how full that cat's stomach was of fresh meat, he didn't go far before scampering up a tree.

Many farmers in the area were happy to see that cougar dead. It was a much easier hunt than the bear experience, nonetheless a very special one. In hound hunting, as with all hunting, you take the easy ones when they come along.

A year and a half later, on my wedding day, my wife presented me with a lifesize mount of my big bear. Today, every time I look at him, the vivid memory of one of the most grueling hunts of my life all comes back. On the wall across from the bear is my cougar, a pleasant reminder of how simple a hound hunt can be, but rarely is.

Hound hunting is not for everyone, but I love everything about it. Watching the dogs work and the passion true houndsmen have for their sport is far different than other forms of hunting, which is what makes it so special. The concerted effort required between man and dog to choreograph a successful hunt on another animal is truly remarkable to watch unfold. Being pushed to the limits, conquering land and harsh elements to achieve a common goal is what hunting is often about. Hunting motivates us to succeed and never give up. Hunting teaches us about ourselves; it teaches us about life.

Chapter 11:

The Newest Whitetail Deer

They're one of the country's greatest conservation success stories, but never did I think I'd have the opportunity to hunt Columbia whitetails in my home state of Oregon.

Approaching the knob we wanted to glass from for the evening, it soon became obvious we would not make it all the way there. Hard ground and brown oak leaves crunching beneath every step, made for slow, noisy going. The air was calm, and sounds carried – we didn't want to risk spooking any deer.

"Let's slowly work our way up to that next oak tree and glass from there," whispered an eager Lee Sandberg, Black Oak Outfitter's top guide. But before we could make it, Lee froze in mid-stride. Nodding his cap to the right, toward a small oak-studded knob, a little buck fed on fallen acorns, less than 100 yards away. The buck's presence forced us to stop in our tracks.

Over the course of the next 20 minutes, three more bucks would join him. The first buck we spotted was a small 8-pointer, not a shooter, not this early in the hunt. Two of the others appeared to be good ones, but through the low-hanging limbs and tall, brown grass, we couldn't get a clear look. One had long tines and good mass, but we couldn't see all of what we needed to in order to call the shot.

With our attention focused on those bucks, it caught me off-guard when a forked-horn stood staring, 75 yards below us in a small gully. Seconds later a dandy, mature 9-pointer joined him. He looked good through the binoculars and even better with the apex of my Trijicon scope cranked on 10x and tucked tight behind his shoulder.

He would have taped out over 110 inches, a good Columbia whitetail buck by any means, and one I probably should have taken. Lee left the decision in my hands. He'd been seeing bigger bucks in the area, but these are whitetails, and you never know what the next day may hold. I had four days left to hunt, and felt we could do better.

It was early September, 2006, and I was hunting just east of Roseburg, Oregon. This is a serious hunting and fishing community, nestled in one of Oregon's most fertile stretches of land, the North Umpqua River Valley. It's here that the rugged Cascade Mountains transition into broken hill country, dominated by hardwood stands of oak.

On the valley floor, rolling hills meet the lush river bottom, in one of the West's most clear-flowing, striking streams. This is where Ernest Hemingway and Zane Grey loved spending time on the water, and once you lay your eyes upon it, you'll understand why. It's this valley that Columbia whitetail deer call home, and where we focused our hunting efforts.

October of 2005 marked the first hunt for Oregon's Columbia whitetail deer in more than a quarter-century; the 2006 season was the second. Sound management and cooperative efforts by land owners and groups such as Safari Club International and the Oregon Hunters Association helped make this long-awaited adventure a reality for many hunters around the world. Their efforts have literally brought this deer back from the brink of extinction.

While steelhead fishing as a boy, I used to love watching Columbia whitetails along the banks of the North Umpqua River. Never did I think I'd one day have the opportunity to hunt them.

LIFE IN THE SCOPE: THE WEST

The Columbia whitetail deer is the westernmost representative of some 30 subspecies of whitetails in North and Central America. Having been under federal protection since 1978, they are a prime example of how sound management, cooperative landowners, volunteer groups, hunting organizations and hunters can all work together to help conserve and promote the perpetuation of a big game species.

It's estimated that more than 6,000 Columbia whitetails call the Umpqua River Basin home, and hopefully that number will continue to grow. Over the course of the next couple of days on my hunt, I'd see several deer, including some good bucks, but they weren't the quality of bucks I'd passed up on the first evening. We did see one, high, heavy 9-point, one I would have liked to have taken, but with the wind and noisy ground, there was no prayer of getting close enough for a shot.

On the second evening of my hunt, we hunted a nearby river bottom. This point of picturesque land is surrounded by the North Umpqua River, with both oak and Douglas fir trees lining the banks. Roaring riffles, a series of rugged waterfalls and attention-getting rapids not only make this stretch of river unique, but it keeps deer in the brushy shoreline habitat. Between the trees and underbrush, there's enough cover to hide plenty of whitetails, and the only way to get them is to sit and wait, patiently.

By nightfall, with our backsides pitched against the base of an old oak tree, we'd see over 50 deer, including some good bucks, but no shooters. Temperatures soared into the lower 80s that day, unseasonably warm by a margin of nearly 20 degrees. This caused the deer to move early and late in the day, and our hunting efforts emulated that, accordingly.

The following morning found us in position high on a hillside, glassing another good buck. We couldn't reach a shooting position due to dry, noisy ground and thick groves of poison oak which separated us. Rather than risk spooking him, we backed out and looked for another deer, planning to return there in the evening with the hopes of locating him in a more approachable position.

Later that morning we found some good Columbia blacktail bucks, including a nice 4x4 that made me think very seriously about shooting. Both the Columbia whitetails and Columbia blacktails overlap in this region of Oregon, and the whitetail tags are good for either species.

That evening we failed to see our buck pop out on the hillside, so we headed back down to the river bottom. We'd see over 40 deer on this night, including some good 6 and 7 pointers we didn't see the previous night. But Lee was adamant about them not being any of the big bucks he knew were in the area.

With one day to go in my hunt, I began regretting not tagging out on that 9-pointer we saw the first evening. There I was, hunting the coveted Columbia whitetail, now one of the most sought after deer subspecies in all of North America, and I was doing it a mere hour's drive from my home.

A year prior to my hunt, my wife, Tiffany, held one of the first tags issued for Columbia whitetails. We were hunting with good friend and fellow outdoor writer, Gary Lewis, who helped arrange the hunts. Gary took as good a buck as you could ever ask for. Though we worked hard for five days to get Tiffany a buck, nothing we saw was worth pulling the trigger on and she went home empty-handed. I felt my hunt was destined for the same ending.

During my wife's hunt, good friend and fellow author, Gary Lewis, tagged this handsome Columbia whitetail while hunting with Black Oak Outfitters.

Overall, these little deer occupy a small area, barely more than 300 square miles. Hunts range from 400 feet in elevation along the river bottom, to over 3,500 feet in the foothills of the adjacent Cascade Range. It's this type of varied terrain which makes hunting these western whitetails so uncertain, so alluring.

On the last morning of my hunt, Lee made certain we got an early start. "I want to be down by the river well before daylight, to see if anything is coming out of the meadows," he insisted. "If there's nothing there, we'll move up and glass the hills, either way, it won't take long to figure out what's out there."

I could sense the urgency in Lee's voice. After all, it was the final day of the season.

Lee was right on target with his prediction. As dawn started to break, dark shadows pocked the meadows lining the North Umpqua River below us. Closer inspection revealed they were deer, but it was still too dark to tell what we had in front of us, blacktails or whitetails.

Minutes slowly passed, and as a trio of deer moved, there was no doubting the stature of the biggest. His chest was thick, with a domineering walk that screamed "big buck." The best part, it was a whitetail.

The moment I saw his rack through the scope, I knew he was one I wanted. No, he wasn't as big as the buck I'd let get away minutes into the hunt, but he was older, with more character.

His rack spanned to the tips of his ears, and his heavy eye-guards told of his age. The symmetry of his 8-point rack really stood out, along with all the corrugations at the base of his antlers. Even in low light conditions, the distinctive white rings around his eyes were easy to see.

Lee stayed put while I used the broken hill country to move in for a closer shot. It didn't take long, and using poison oak thickets, groves of oak trees and some undulating ground, I soon found myself belly-crawling into final shooting position.

Trying not to alert the buck to my presence, I stayed low until the very last moment, hoping he'd be there when I reached my predetermined point. Thankfully, right where I popped up, a rise in the ground provided the perfect rest. Nestling the forend of the rifle atop the dirt mound, while at the same time parting dry grass, I cranked the Trijicon to full power.

Finding the buck in the scope was easy, and as he raised his head and stopped moving from right to left, I eased back the hammer on my one-shot rifle, ready to take the 130 yard shot. At the crack of the gun, the buck lunged forward, staggered 40 yards and piled up.

On the final day of the hunt I was able to connect on this beautiful Columbia whitetail, the newest and most prized member of the whitetail hunting world at the time.

Making the moment even more special, the famed North Umpqua River, the one I'd lived so many cherished moments on since boyhood, provided the backdrop. From where the buck fell I could stand and see where I'd taken steelhead, salmon, turkey and blacktail deer.

Finally, my dream of tagging a trophy Columbia whitetail came to fruition. Ever since I was a kid growing up in this region, I'd always wanted to hunt these grand little deer, and quite honestly, never thought I'd have the chance.

Will I ever hunt Columbia whitetails again? I'd like to think so, but more than anything I'd like others to experience what I was so fortunate to live out. If conservation efforts continue to prosper and if deer populations continue to expand, then perhaps I will hunt them again. If not, I'm content in knowing that I had at least one opportunity to pursue one of the greatest animals in all of North America.

Chapter 12:

The One That Got Away

Not all hunts end in success. On this mule deer hunt, just about everything that could go wrong, did, including having a big buck being shot out from underneath us.

Glassing the badlands below, it was only a matter of minutes until we found the buck we wanted. He was a high, heavy 4x4 mule deer the outfitter had been watching for more than a month. It was November 12th, opening day of the 2005 rifle season in this section of northwestern South Dakota, and my wife, Tiffany, held a prized tag.

"He'll push the 170-inch mark," noted Reese Clarkson of Mill Iron Outfitters. "He's one of three big bucks that have been hanging out in this area over the past several weeks. You'll know him when you see him."

Dubbed the Devil's Half Acre, it's not because of it's small size that the pocket of badlands we hunted got it's name, rather due to the rugged terrain which was a harsh contrast to the docile farmland above. It's prototypical mule deer habitat, and one that can eat up the better part of a day trying to simply locate a buck.

But such was not the case on this day, as the big buck emanated from a deep ravine, chasing does with only one thing on his mind. The rut was in full-swing, and the fact our target buck was the first buck we'd seen, made the day seem promising.

However, the conditions were poor, not for hunting in general, but for hunting the way were going about it. Our intent was to capture the hunt on film for Limbsaver Outdoors TV show. Thirty-five mile per hour winds and driving rains kept us from getting out of the truck. Bad weather and TV cameras don't mix, and often times we simply can't film in treacherous conditions like this. Having a camera break down in the middle of our season would not be a good thing.

After watching the big buck for two hours, he finally melted into the deep cut banks and labyrinth of washouts which make up the Devil's Half Acre. Figuring he was safely tucked away in the heart of Clarkson's little piece of paradise, we decided to pull out, returning once the storm subsided. That buck hadn't budged from the Half Acre for several weeks, and we all felt confident he'd spend the day in there.

Driving to another area, we soon came across a bedded muley holding tight against a vertical bank, out of the wind and somewhat protected from the rain. While evaluating the massive buck through the spotting scope, there's no doubt he was a shooter. His bases were among the heaviest I've seen anywhere on a mule deer, and his height was well into the mid 20s. However, with a spread of about 17 inches, and the fact he was a 3x3, Tiffany decided to pass. "Let's see what the weather does, I'd really like to get that big buck," she decided.

Tiffany has hunted with me off and on over the years, but recently, the responsibilities of raising a family has taken priority over her hunting endeavors. In fact, this was the first time in five years she'd been away from our two sons, now ages five and three. We knew the boys were in good hands with Grandma and Grandpa, but still, our intent was to have a quick turnaround on this hunt so Tiffany could get back to them.

Clarkson's properties had not been hunted for seven years, and the number and quality of big bucks convey that. Intent to focus on archery hunting, it was a blessing Tiffany even had the opportunity to hunt this land. Clarkson invited Tiffany to apply for a rifle tag, and she drew, something that's not easy for a nonresident to do. A neighboring outfitter of Clarkson's had 12 nonresident rifle hunters apply, and zero drew.

Clarkson's family has been in this part of South Dakota since the 1800s, and as a working cattle and sheep rancher, he intimately knows every inch of land and the animals that live there. Prior to Tiffany's arrival, I spent five days bowhunting the area with Clarkson. At one point I had Tiffany's target deer within 40 yards, but he wouldn't stop walking, thus I never had a shot opportunity. At the time, I was actually happy, for I wanted Tiffany to get this fine deer. Reese and I actually watched this buck every day of my hunt, making sure we knew where he roamed.

If there was ever a slam-dunk mule deer hunt to be had on a short timeline, this was it, or so we thought. In fact, we were so confident Tiffany would get this buck in a day of hunting, that we had her fly in to Rapid City late in the evening, planned on her hunting the next day, then hopping back on the plane at noon the following morning. Had it not been for the torrential downpour and high winds, the hunt would have ended within the first hour. Then the situation really took a turn for the worst.

Toward mid-afternoon, a hole in the approaching clouds provided a glimmer of hope. Confident it was the break we needed, we hustled back over to the Half Acre. Several minutes passed, and to everyone's surprise, the big buck was nowhere to be found.

Mill Iron's top guide, Scott Koan, had joined us, and even his muley-magnet eyes couldn't pick up the buck. But he did find something interesting. "Hey, take a look through the spotting scope; he's not the big one, but he'll be of interest to you," Koan whispered.

With the spotting scope cranked to full-power, a gray muzzle and white set of antlers filled the lens. All I could do was smile. The distinct face, wide rack and deteriorating physique of the monarch said it all. This was the same mule deer buck we'd seen when I was bowhunting the same area some six weeks prior. I'd failed to fill my tag then, so was back, trying to finish the job, which I did after Tiffany returned home.

The first time we saw this old buck, he was on another property, less than 100 yards from Clarkson's place. We waited out the buck, hoping he'd cross into the Half Acre but he never did. In fact, that was the last anyone had seen of him, until now.

As Tiffany peeked at her potential prize, she was all for going after him. He was a magnificent looking buck full of character. Just then, Reese spotted a vehicle on the county road, a good mile from where we sat. We watched as the poachers poked a barrel out the window and shot a small forked horn from the road, on a piece of private property. Reese immediately called the land owner, who sped out and handled the incident.

Disgusted at the act we'd just witnessed, it put a sour taste in all of our mouths. Fortunately for us, the old muley was still in the bottom of the canyon, and the weather was holding good. Taking off on foot, the going was slow. Following the intense rain, the gumbo mud which we had no choice but to walk through, was like treading on ice. Not only was it slippery, but it stuck to our boots, adding several pounds of extra weight to each foot. It made for slow, clumsy walking, forcing us to frequently stop and clear our boots of the cement-like mud.

As we finally drew closer, Tiffany got to take a better look at the buck. "He looks so old, not like the other deer we've been seeing," she noticed. "Let's go get him."

That's all we needed to hear before jumping into the heart of the Half Acre. Reese knows every draw, ridge and cut-bank of the Half Acre like the floorplan of his own home, and felt confident he could get Tiffany within 75 yards for a clear shot. More than an hour passed, and just as I laid the pack across a slippery mud ledge for Tiffany to rest her gun on, a shot rang out from above us.

At the report of the rifle, the wide, heavy-framed 4-point bolted, never to be seen again. For us it was strike two. As if the ice-cold morning rains weren't enough to put a damper on what should have been an easy hunt, this time another trespasser ruined a prized opportunity at a trophy muley. The hunter had shot a doe, which he had a tag for, but he did it on the wrong property, Clarkson's property. A call to the sheriff, who just happened to be Reese's father, and another court case was in the making.

Dejected, we left the Half Acre with no sign of the original buck we'd hoped to have on the ground by now. Searching for something positive, we looked to a young girl to help turn things around. Joining us on this day was Dani Koan, Scott's 12 year old daughter. Dani is a passionate hunter, and has been since she was a small child. This season she'd already taken her first elk and antelope, and she, too, held a mule deer tag.

These rifle tags are easier for residents to draw than nonresidents. Our original plan was to have Tiffany get her buck, then film Dani hunting her first mule deer. Hoping to turn things around, we decided to try and go find a buck for Dani.

"There are a couple of big super-twos in one drainage," Scott Koan shared. "They are full-grown bucks, and they're never going to get any better than forkys. We've been watching them for a few years now, and there's no question we need to take them out of the gene pool. Let's go see if we can get Dani one of those bucks."

It was a stressful day, and this sounded like the perfect solution to help remedy the somber mood. As we neared the base of a big draw, Scott pointed to where a couple of the big super-twos had been bedding in the broken ravines, then coming out to feed in the evening.

No sooner had we rounded a corner and there stood a band of does, one of which was being chased by the biggest of the forked-horn bucks. As Dani, her dad and camera man, Bret Stuart, stealthed their way to within comfortable shooting range, the 20-plus-inch wide buck had not a care in the world. He was so preoccupied with the does, it allowed the hunters to move across the wide open terrain, to within 130 yards.

Despite the intensity of the moment, Dani remained calm and was in total control. Patiently she waiting for the buck to turn broadside and stop. Finally, the shot opportunity came and she didn't skip a beat. Placing the

Twelve year old Dani Koan added a bright light to an otherwise dismal day when she took this, her first mule deer.

bullet where she wanted it, the buck humped up then slowly edged forward, tumbling down over an embankment. That quickly transformed a dark day into a brighter one.

"Hey, let's take care of this buck and get over to where Tiffany's buck is," Scott urged. "We still have about 30 minutes of daylight and maybe we can at least see where he is so we know where to start in the morning."

Hurriedly, we dressed out Dani's buck then hightailed it over to the Half Acre. Pulling up to glass, four does moved out of the breaks and into an alfalfa field. Deer had been feeding here for weeks, and the big buck was consistently making his way into the field over the past week to check out the does.

Sure enough, right behind the does came Tiffany's big buck. They were in Clarkson's field, just as they had been for several consecutive evenings. Things were looking up.

With Tiffany's buck following the does across the big field, we figured we could slip along a fence, get into a ditch line and hustle to within shooting range before nightfall. But the buck kept pushing the does, and there was no catching up.

He was on them so hard, they waned from their normal routine of stopping to feed. Instead they kept moving, and at 800 yards out, the does jumped a fence, one-by-one, on to a neighboring property. The buck followed and seconds after disappearing into a ravine, a shot rang out.

Back across the fence came the four does, followed shortly by the buck. Noticeably he'd been hit, and when he stopped, another shot rang out. This time the buck went on the run, moving out of sight over a knoll in the field. Moments later a hunter appeared, standing at the fence line.

"I shot a buck on our side of the...." he started as we approached him. We confided that we'd seen the whole thing, and knew it was a legal act. "I just

The buck that got away, at least from my wife, Tiffany. This was one of the lowest moments of my professional hunting career, for all that could go wrong, did.

wanted to get permission to cross the fence so I could go finish him off." Not a problem.

Accompanying the man on to Clarkson's property, we moved into the gully where we'd last seen the deer. A final shot put the big buck down for good, Tiffany's buck. He was the buck Clarkson had been watching for over a month; the same buck we watched all morning that we all desperately wanted Tiffany to get. It was one of the lowest points of my entire hunting career, not because someone else had shot it, but because of the way the day had went. Bad weather, TV cameras and poachers all played a roll in that buck being killed by another hunter. But that's hunting.

As for Tiffany, she took it well, accepting the fact that anything can happen in fair chase hunting. She's hunted enough to realize that.

The hunter who scored on the big buck was Jim Eldringhoff, a South Dakota resident who was hunting on the neighboring land. Jim could have shot this buck several times when it was on the wrong side of the fence, but held out for him to cross. He could have jumped the fence and started firing, once it had been hit, but chose to wait. Everything Jim did was by the book, the way it should be. It was a positive point in an otherwise gloomy day.

It was a restless night of sleep, especially for Tiffany. She wanted that big buck, as we all did. Up early the next morning, we headed back to the Devil's Half Acre in search of the old buck and two other big muleys that had been hanging out there. The hole was empty, a result of all the disturbance the previous day.

Heading back to where we'd seen the high, heavy 3-point the day prior, he now became our target. A quick scan of the country revealed nothing, then Koan sighted another high-racked 3x3. Tiffany took one look at the buck and made no hesitation. "Let's try for him!"

Clarkson and Koan picked out the best path for us to take to get within shooting range, then turned Tiffany, myself and the camera man loose. Working our way through dried creek beds, we popped up over a knoll, confident the buck would be within 75 yards of us. When we peeked over the rim, however, nothing could be seen. "We've gone too far," I whispered, "let's backtrack and head up that other little draw."

Now in the right place, peering over the rise, we could see the tips of the buck's antlers, right where we'd last seen him. Popping up the shooting sticks, Tiff' took a firm rest. Pulling back the hammer on her Thompson Center .270, she quickly got the buck in her scope. Just then he started to move, showing interest in a doe that was with him.

Three hours before boarding a plane, Tiffany connected on this South Dakota mule deer. It was a positive end to a mentally taxing hunt.

Changing position, Tiffany reset the sticks and again, got on the buck. The buck was moving into a grassy draw, and in a few steps he'd be out of sight. With no time to spare, she took the only shot she had. The Remington 130 grain Swift Scirocco bullet found its mark on the spine, behind the shoulder, dropping the buck in his tracks.

For Tiffany it was her first mule deer, marking the end to a perfect spot and stalk hunt. Though it wasn't the buck she'd hoped for, it was a positive way to close the hunt, and we had some great eating meat for the family to enjoy.

Within a few hours of pulling the trigger, Tiffany was on a plane back home. There are plenty of big bucks still roaming this region. Perhaps one day Tiffany will draw another limited tag and get a shot at making her South Dakota big buck dreams come true.

Chapter 13:

Kodiak Island Blacktails

Not only do I consider Sitka blacktails to be the most beautiful deer in North America – arguably, the world – but they are also the tastiest eating. On these hunts, I got the best of both worlds... big bucks and plenty of good meat.

Making my way to the highest point of land within a three mile radius, the plan was to crest the ridge and hunt the opposite hillside. Nearing the top, movement in a thick willow patch caught my eye. Further inspection through my 10x40 binoculars revealed a good Sitka buck, but there was no way of threading a shot through the tangled mess, especially once he bedded down.

Trying to escape the howling wind, I edged around the backside of the knob, hoping to get a shot when the deer stood. A change in wind direction tipped off the deer and he slipped out of the jam through a well worn escape route he had etched into the tall, brown grass surrounding his lair.

Twelve hours in the field with several miles of ground covered, he was one of only two bucks I'd see on this, the first day of my 2002 Kodiak Island deer hunt. It was dark by the time I reached the tiny bay in which our boat sat moored off of Uganik Passage. When the five members of our hunting party reconvened, it was evident our game plan would take some revamping, as the biggest bucks were hanging on the highest points of land, not near the beaches as we'd hoped.

At daybreak the next morning, good friend Art Peck and myself would run two buddies down the beach by skiff, allowing them to spend four days hunting their way back to the big boat. The rest of us would spread out, covering as much high ground as possible. Initially, it sounded like a failsafe plan.

In the short time it took to gather the gear, load the skiff and start down the bay, a storm developed. Before we knew it, three-foot whitecaps were breaking over the bow of the skiff. In our rush to beat the storm, the bilge pump was forgotten, an oversight that nearly cost us our lives.

Incessant winds prevented us from making it to the designated drop point, 10 miles down the beach. Avoiding the breakers close to shore, Art maneuvered the skiff into bigger waters, trying to buck the wind as best he could. The three of us laid flat on the bottom of the inflatable raft, dispersing the weight of our bodies and packs to keep the craft from flipping over in the gale force winds. Eight inches of water stood in the skiff, but we dared not shift any weight for fear of capsizing.

In a bold move to prevent us from traveling further to sea, Art abruptly pivoted the boat 180 degrees, working us back toward land. Though we took on major wakes, it was our only hope out of the life-threatening situation. Hitting a gravel beach, our buddies hopped out, the majority of their gear drenched. Dropping them off as originally planned was our only hope. Had they remained in the boat, too much weight would have made for a grim outlook, and given the fact any shifting of mass would likely tip the boat, bailing water by hand was not a smart move.

Soaking wet with no survival gear aboard, waiting out the storm in a semi-protected cove was not an option. Art and I had to return to the main boat, where the fifth member of our party awaited. Traveling with the fierce wind, whitecaps outran us, filling the boat from behind. At this point I had no option but to start bailing water. With the aid of a paddle, I frantically splashed out some 300 hundred pounds of water while Art held the kicker at full throttle. My numbed hands slowly regained their dexterity amid the intense bailing session while my pulse rate dramatically escalated, fearing death was not out of touch.

What should have taken no more than 30 minutes to complete the round-trip drop-off, ate up nearly two hours before Art and I made it back to the mother ship. In one of the worst storms to hit Kodiak Island that year, three of us were stuck in the main boat for two more days. Wind gusts in excess of 100 miles per hour were registered and all we could do was pray the anchor would hold in the tiny bay we were in.

Our buddies spent the two days tucked in a tent beneath a small stand of spruce trees, 50 yards from where we dropped them. It was their goal to stay alive by keeping warm, and given the fact all of their gear, sleeping bags included, were wet, this would not be an easy task.

Once the storm ceased, we went back to hunting. This is Alaska, where one minute you're facing death, the next you're enjoying the stunning land and all it has to offer

At the end of the day, no one had seen a a single deer. On day five of the hunt, the weather broke and for the first time azure skies greeted us. Cruising the shoreline in our skiff, Art caught glimpse of a fleeting doe in tall grass, high atop a hillside. Close inspection revealed a buck was in hot pursuit, and he was worth a better look. Quietly tying off the skiff, a hike to the top of the little knoll found us in prime position.

A respectable forked horn first showed himself, but he was not the one we were after. Then a heavy racked, big necked buck emerged from beneath a frond of alders. A grizzled muzzle stood out in stark contrast to an ebony forehead. His massive size caught me off-guard, for his live weight would no doubt tip the scales to 170 pounds.

At 150 yards, I settled in for the uphill shot. Using Art's 7mm-08 which he himself custom made, the petite five pound gun fit nicely into the crook of my shoulder. Resting my cheek on the smooth Western big leaf maple stock, the gun roared with the slightest of finger pressure. The 160 grain bullet put the buck down.

The deer sported a heavy 3x4 rack, though one of his eye guards had been severed in battle. He was a handsome deer, and wasting no time getting him off the hill, out of brown bear range and into the skiff, I was more than

I think Sitka blacktails are among the world's most beautiful deer. This, my first buck off Kodiak Island, came following a rebound of deer populations that had been hit hard by harsh winters. I was fortunate to get him.

pleased to have this, one of only two buck's we'd end up with on this trip.

In 2006 I returned to hunt blacktails on Kodiak Island. By this time, buck populations were higher than when I'd previously hunted them. Mild winters and fruitful springs allowed the animals to rebound from the harsh winters of 1998 and 1999, when a high percentage of deer perished across the island.

On this hunt I was on a charter boat out of Larsen Bay, on the northwest side of the island. Good friend and noted Kenai River fishing guide, Greg Brush, helped arrange this hunt. Our objective was to get two TV shows from our sojourn, one for Outdoor America, one for Western Adventures. Greg's young teenage daughter, Kelsey, a hunting maniac, was also on this trip.

The first morning of the hunt couldn't have gotten off to a better start. Snow was falling, adding to the nearly 10-inches that already blanketed the ground. When it comes to hunting trophy bucks in late November on Kodiak Island, snow is the hunter's best friend. This is what it takes to drive the older bucks from the high country to more accessible land.

From the big boat my camera man, Bret Stuart, and I glassed more than 20 deer, two of which were dandy bucks. Laying out our options, we came up with a game plan. It was comforting hunting with Bret; he's a great hunter, an extremely hard worker and willing to go to the extremes to get the job done. He's the kind of friend you trust your life with, possessing several life skills I wish I had. He's the kind of man you can give a shovel to and he'll build a snow mobile out of it if you want him too. I was sad when Bret had to leave the filming occupation and move on to other ventures.

Having the captain drop Bret and I on shore, we planned on meeting him at the same spot, just before dark. Late November on Kodiak Island doesn't leave much in the way of daylight, so we wasted no time.

Pushing through a few small draws and willow thickets, Bret and I were amazed at the amount of deer sign we were seeing. Plenty of does were around, along with a few smaller bucks.

Then we reached the perfect location. Two big draws merged into one larger drainage, and deer trails were everywhere. Four primary trails intersected in the only open meadow around, an area about half the size of a football field. Studying the terrain, wind direction and the amount of rubs and feeding sign that was near, I made the decision to break out the grunt tube and rattle bag.

While Bret got the camera set on the tripod, I began rattling. Snow fell hard, but it was a dry, quiet snow. Visibility was barely 75 yards, less in some directions. Rattling from the northern edge of the clearing, I hoped to pull a buck from the south side, where the thickest grove of willows were located.

Generating another sequence of sounds from the synthetic rattle bag, all felt good. My only concern was that the heavy snow would dampen the sound of the rattle bag, not allowing it to reach it's full potential, volume wise. A grunt here and there, followed by another 15 minutes of rattling, and still I felt positive despite the fact no deer came running to the sounds.

Figuring the sound wasn't reaching far enough, Bret and I decided to relocate and try again. Just as I stood, a stud of a buck came bolting out of the brush, right where I'd hoped.

He paused on the very edge of the dark willows, making it tough to decipher his chocolate colored rack. Between the heavy falling snow and the tangled backdrop of the willows, I simply couldn't tell how big he was, even though he was only 70 yards away.

Despite being the end of November, Kodiak's brown bears left no question they were still roaming the land in search of food. Such sign takes deer hunting to a whole new level.

The buck stood, intently looking our direction, but I don't think he saw us. Needing to get a better look, I hit the grunt tube, hoping he'd shift his head. Instead, he started prancing right at us.

At 60 yards the buck began skirting around us, and for the first time I got a look at his magnificent rack. A perfect 4x4, heavy framed brute was more than I'd expected. Glancing back at Bret, he nodded his head, indicating the camera was on the deer.

With my .300 resting solidly in the shooting sticks, the buck loomed larger and larger through the strikingly clear, Trijicon scope. The moment he paused, I let him have it. He dropped on the spot.

Wanting to avoid taking a second shot for fear of attracting brown bears, I was relieved to see the buck crumble so quickly. There are many instances on Kodiak Island where hunters have taken a second or third shot at their deer, and the brown bears homed in on the sounds. The bear interpret the shots as somewhat of a dinner bell, associating them with a dead deer, thus easy food. Fighting a brown bear off this kill was the last thing I wanted to do.

Dragging the buck into the middle of the snow-covered meadow, we admired his heavy, dark rack. He taped out at 105-inches, enough to make the awards book for Boone & Crockett, had I elected to enter him.

My best Sitka blacktail came in hard to a rattle bag during a snow storm on Kodiak Island. I'll be hard-pressed to find a better buck than this record-class brute.

With the gun loaded, Bret watched for bears while I skinned and boned the deer. We were seeing some gigantic bear tracks in the area, proof that not all the brownies had retreated to their winter dens. Once the smell of dead deer hits the air, there's no telling what might happen on Kodiak Island.

In short order I had the buck boned out and his head removed. The tedious job of caping I'd finish in more comfort, on the boat. Stuffing some of the meat, head and cape into my pack, Bret took the bulk of the meat in his pack. We were loaded down, but were able to get every bit of meat and the head out in one trip.

For those who have never hunted Kodiak Island, the Sitka deer I'd just killed was the true buck of a lifetime. I know several folks who have hunted Kodiak for over 20 years and not taken bucks this big. Believe me, I knew what I had and was counting my blessings. The chances of my ever taking a buck this big again on Kodiak are very slim, and I knew that the minute I walked up on this grand buck. Without a doubt, he was one of the greatest trophy class animals I'd ever taken in North America.

Greg and Kelsey Brush with a pair of Sitka blacktails taken from the same spot. The fact both shots were caught on film made the experience that much more special.

I never tire of hunting Kodiak Island. The adventure it offers, the ever looming uncertainties, the captivating scenery and it's very special animals all go to make it one of the most unique hunting destinations on the planet.

From there, the rest of the trip was a joy. I ended up spot and stalking my way to a second buck, and we caught Greg and his daughter Kelsey on film, each shooting a buck.

In all, we had six members in our hunting party, and took 24 deer. All the hunters but me were residents, looking to get meat for their freezers. On the last day, one of the hunters took a buck even bigger than mine, a dandy four point scoring into the high 'teens. It was his first deer hunt ever. What an animal to start with.

For me, hunting Kodiak Island blacktails is something I can never get enough of. The land is overpowering with it's ruggedness and vast beauty. It's animals command respect like no other place can. Feasting on fresh venison and crab meat each night was better than any five star restaurant I'd ever dined in. Sharing it all with good friends made the success and fond memories that much more vivid.

Chapter 14:

Lone Star Mule Deer

When I was first invited on this Texas hunt,
I was reluctant to accept...then I learned the hunt was for
mule deer, not whitetails. Count me in!

We were in position well before daylight, ready to glass the breaks where a pair of big mule deer bucks had been seen. Cal Ferguson, owner of 4F Outfitters in the northern most section of the Texas panhandle, assured me the bucks were in there as he'd seen them just a couple days prior, on his final scouting trip to the area.

When asked just how big these bucks were, Cal simply replied, "You'll know when you see them, they dwarf everything else in this area." That was good enough for me.

As darkness gave way to daylight, we stayed high, searching for deer in the coulees and labyrinth of cut banks meandering through the rather flat landscape. From a distance, the land looked nothing like mule deer habitat. Flat, open terrain for as far as the eye could see in every direction. With cotton and grass fields constituting the surrounding farmland, it seemed more like whitetail country than anything.

Then we saw our first muley buck. He was a 140 class 4x4, not worth a second look according to Ferguson. "The two bucks we're looking for have been hanging together in this area since summer; they have to be around here, somewhere," stated an optimistic Ferguson as he continued glassing.

It was early December and in this part of Texas, that marks the mule deer rut – it wasn't by accident we were hunting at this time. But on this, our first day of the hunt, something happened, a change in nature which fouled things.

The temperature had dropped more than 40 degrees overnight, and the high-powered winds blew rain, sleet and snow horizontally across the desert all day long. The horrendous weather lasted until dark, and we saw only a fraction of the deer we'd expected.

Jason Hart, a buddy from the east coast, was also in camp, searching for his first muley. He hunted an area a few miles away, in the hill country. The weather was bad there too, but the big cliffs, rocky bluffs and deep ravines afforded the deer a degree of protection from the harsh elements.

"As soon as we got there, we saw a buck chasing a doe," recalls Hart. "Watching the buck chase this doe was one of the most awesome things I'd ever seen. He wouldn't leave her for anything. Every time she moved, he'd throw his head down and follow, not letting her out of his sight."

Hart's guide, Clint Ferguson, Cal's brother, told me he was an average buck for that area. "He wasn't too intent to have me shoot this buck, but the more we watched him, the more I wanted him," Hart grinned.

As the buck pushed does deeper into a ravine, the hunting duo made a plan to get above the deer and stalk down. It worked, and soon Hart was in shooting position. The fact the buck had some chipped points off his 4x4 rack didn't matter a bit to Hart, who already had his mind made up.

At the shot, the buck went down, and soon Hart was admiring his first ever

My good friend, Jason Hart, traveled from his home on the East Coast to take this, his first mule deer. He couldn't have been more pleased with his Texas buck. Unfortunately, shortly after returning home, the rack was stolen from his porch... he never saw it again.

mule deer. "I know he's not as big of a deer as we probably could have got, but I don't care," smiled Hart. "Just watching that buck and all he represented; it was just like what I'd read about, hunting mule deer like this out West. The setting couldn't have been more beautiful, the deer were so majestic. Everything just seemed right, so I took him. It's a hunt I'll never forget."

Though I spent the entire day looking for the two bucks, the big boys were nowhere to be seen. We returned the next morning and at daylight were in position, once again glassing, first the agricultural land, then the breaks. The weather had changed, still cold, but not the biting wind and blowing snow we'd experienced the day prior.

The conditions seemed perfect, one of those crisp, cool mornings you'd think would find bucks chasing does in every pocket. But it wasn't the case. We covered a great deal of ground that day, glassing, walking, breaking out the spotting scopes, doing all we could to locate the pair of bucks.

We did see some bucks, obviously with does on their minds, but nothing over 150 inches. Our target bucks were much larger than that. "The smaller of the two will go about 170, just a bit over," shared Cal, revealing for the first time just how big these bucks really were. "The other one is quite a bit bigger, in the lower 190s."

Cal didn't want to get my hopes up, wishing that I could see for myself just how big the bucks were. I knew there were 170 class bucks around, even bigger ones, but knowing the true size of the bigger buck in the area...let's just say it got my attention.

The thought of seeing such a big buck inspired me, and after Cal shared photos of some of the bigger bucks in the area – both on the hoof and those taken by previous hunters – I really got excited. Though we failed to see the big bucks, my optimism had never been higher. Every time we popped over a rise or skirted around a point to glass the land, I tried willing the deer to be there, but to no avail.

We did see one good buck, a 160 class 4x4, but not a shooter knowing the big bucks could be around the next corner. It was mid-day, and we decided to watch this buck as he worked hard to keep his group of more than a dozen does under control. He'd chase one doe here, another there, but when he tried retaining a girl about 200 yards from the herd, up a creek bed, he quickly retreated, another buck tight on his tail.

No, it wasn't one of the big muleys we were looking for, rather a fat-racked whitetail. The muley made his way back to the harem, and tried standing his ground. As the bucks locked in battle, their activity carried them out of sight, and we never saw who won; not until later that afternoon.

We moved on, searching for our big bucks, but our efforts revealed nothing. Backtracking through the terrain we'd covered earlier in the day, we came upon the group of mule deer does where the fight had taken place. Laying smack in the middle of the bedded herd was who else but the big whitetail buck. He'd won the battle, taking over the entire harem of mule deer does – the muley buck was nowhere to be seen.

Day two ended without a glimpse of the big bucks, but our spirits remained high. We covered all the ground where those two big bucks could have been, and flat-out failed to find them. Had they moved out of the area or were they hiding? My money was on the former.

All the other bucks in the area, including several of the youngsters, were hot on does, and if the big bucks were around, they wouldn't have tolerated it. Why they moved out remained the biggest question in my mind. There were does, and plenty of them throughout the area. Were there other does further along in their estrous cycles which may have lured the big bucks out of the area? Could the severe cold snap have forced them to move out? And if it was the bad weather, why did the other bucks stick around?

Trying to sort it out as much as we could, what we surmised made no difference. The bucks weren't around and there wasn't a thing we could do about it.

Day four found us moving to the hill country, a land that reminded me more of the East Cape Province of South Africa than any Texas real estate I'd ever set eyes on. The decision to move was mutual, and as Clint Ferguson and I headed to the hills, a new day brought renewed energy.

It started off well, with a fair four point buck chasing a single doe right in front of us. We climbed just shy of 1,000 feet in elevation above the valley floor we'd been hunting. The altitude change proved to be a good move, for every buck we saw was hot on does. You could feel the new day brought with it a heightened level of optimism.

After looking over a half-dozen decent bucks throughout the day, Clint spotted a good one. "He's only a 3-point, but he's high, wide and very heavy," whispered Ferguson. "It's definitely worth taking the time to get a closer look at him."

Dropping in to a gully, we covered ground fast, hoping to intercept the buck as he intensely worked a trail, obviously searching for receptive does. A half-mile later we eased up through a small saddle, ready for a close look. Nothing. We sat and glassed in all directions and saw only a small 4x4. Ten minutes later the three point buck emerged from out of a brushy creek bottom, about a half-mile distant.

"He's going to hit that trail and work straight away, over into the next drainage," urged Ferguson. "If we want to get a closer look at him, we'll have to hustle."

Hustle we did, for though it was only a half mile to the buck, in order for us to reach him we had to hightail it back from where we came, then cover an additional quarter mile, just to get a look at him. We made it, just in time to see the buck drop into the bottom of the drainage.

"He's about 500 yards from leaving our property; if you want to shoot him, we'll have to hurry," Ferguson urged. To be quite honest, I still was not convinced he was the buck for me, but we decided to make a move, anyway.

A quarter-mile, downhill sprint, hidden the whole time from the moving buck, helped us close the distance. Peeking up over a knoll, we were now inside 400 yards of the buck, the closest we'd been. "He's going to go 25, 26-inches wide, and he does have a little kicker off one side," Clint pointed out.

It was an impressive spread, but what caught my eye was his mass and tine length. He was a huge bodied buck, and given the character of his rack, he was a unique animal. The more I watched him, the more appealing he became.

"What do you think, should we go for it?" I whispered. Clint turned, smiled and raised his eyebrows. That was all the confirmation I needed.

The buck was still on the move, and was quickly approaching the neighboring property, where he'd be off-limits. Running another 200 yards downhill, we crawled up over a rise and I nestled the Thompson Center .270 into a pile of grass and broken shale. A quick reading on the Nikon range finder confirmed the distance at 230 yards.

To date, this Texas buck is the biggest bodied mule deer I'd ever killed. The stalk leading up to the deer was fast-pace and came down to the wire.

Tim Herald took this buck on the final day of our Texas hunt. Since this, our first hunt together, Tim and I have shared several outings

As soon as the buck stopped, I squeezed the trigger and the 130 grain Remington Swift Scirocco bullet was on its way. At the impact, the buck humped up, lunged forward, then fell. With a glowing sun falling below the distant horizon, the setting was absolutely breathtaking. Snapping photos against a fiery sunset, it was an appropriate end to a very memorable hunt.

On the final day of our hunt, good friend, Tim Herald hunted with Cal Ferguson, and I tagged along. Tim is one of the greatest, most honest men in the outdoor industry, and he's the one who arranged this hunt. A few years following this, our first hunt together, Tim and I would serve as cohosts of Outdoor America, on the Outdoor Channel.

Right away Tim and Cal spotted a buck, and Tim knew it was one he wanted. The muley had his harem of does, and as they moved from a brushy flat into a protected bowl, Tim closed in for a shot. One shot from his 7mm dropped the buck. Our Texas mule deer hunt had come to an end, with 100% success.

While Texas is noted as one of the premier whitetail states in the U.S., it receives little attention in the mule deer world. Though many hunters focus their efforts on the Rocky Mountain states and beyond to fulfill their mule deer dreams, don't overlook the Texas Panhandle, it has the potential of producing that dream buck you may have been searching for.

Chapter 15:

Coues Deer Quest

Taking a Coues deer is something any hunter should be proud of, but getting one that makes the record books is a major accomplishment. On this hunt, the efforts of trying to get the kill shot on film almost cost us...almost!

It was January, 2006, and I was hunting in Sonora, Mexico with good friend and noted outfitter, Jeremy Toman. I'd hunted mule deer with Jeremy on this same land, as well as chased brown bear with him out of his Alaska camp. He's one of the hardest working, most knowledgeable men I know, and I love hunting with him.

On this trip, we were working to get a representative Coues deer for a Western Adventures TV show. We were hunting out of Hermosillo, a place that holds a good number of Coues deer, but on average the bucks aren't as big as they are farther to the north. With that in mind, all we looked for was a 3x3 scoring around 90-inches. If I'd had more time to spend chasing these gray desert ghosts, we could have hoped for a bigger buck, but as it was, I would have been more than pleased with a good representative animal. Besides, this was my first Coues deer hunt, and I wasn't about to be too picky.

I had another motive in trying to secure a Coues deer. If I could pull it off, the deer would complete a single-season deer slam, something that had never been done before, or so I'd been told by many authorities.

I'd already taken a Columbia blacktail in Oregon, along with a Sitka blacktail in Alaska. My whitetail was taken in Idaho, and I also shot the newest member in the deer hunting world, the highly prized Columbia whitetail. I'd also taken a few mule deer during the season, both in the Rocky Mountains and in the desert. The only deer species needed to secure a single-season slam was this Coues deer, arguably the hardest of all to attain.

During the first couple days of the hunt we saw a few little bucks but nothing to get too serious about. The weather was unseasonably cold – 40° to 50° cooler than it should have been – which predictably shut down the deer movement. We were a little early to hit the peak of the rut, but were seeing signs of some early rutting activity which kept us hopeful.

One afternoon, late in the hunt, it started to warm up. The sudden weather change not only lifted our mental spirits, it got the deer moving again. In a short time, we saw more Coues deer than we'd seen the three previous days combined. Driving along a road we'd not yet been on, Jeremy motioned for the driver to stop the truck. "Coues buck!" he excitedly whispered.

Nearly 300 yards across a grassy flat, a buck and doe stood near one of the many low-profile bushes pocking the plateau. Before we could get the binoculars on them, the buck bedded down and all we could see was the tip of his rack. "Let's get out slowly, try to make it to that hill over there and see if we can get a closer look at him," Jeremy suggested.

No sooner had we taken a few steps when the deer stood up. I had a shot, and camera man, Bret Stuart, worked fast to get the buck in frame. About the time the camera was ready, the deer bolted. By Toman's reaction I knew it was a good buck, but there was no way of getting a shot on film. It simply happened too fast. "That's one of the biggest Coues bucks I've ever seen on this ranch!" Jeremy exclaimed. "We have to try to get on him again."

Strapping on the packs, we were off and running across the high desert, heading into thick brush where we'd last seen the big deer disappear. Dodging more varieties of cacti than I'd seen in my entire life, within minutes we entered the brushline near where we last saw the buck.

Astonishingly, no sooner had we made it through the brush and into the first opening when, there the buck stood. He was in heavy shadows, just under 300 yards away. I could plainly see the buck, but in the harsh contrast between intense sunlight and black shadows, Bret couldn't find him.

Jeremy was urging me to shoot, and I wanted to in the worst way, but couldn't. "He's going to go over 110-inches," Jeremy squealed. "Just shoot him and we'll make something up! He's the biggest buck I've seen here!"

Unfortunately, filming hunting shows isn't like being on a Hollywood set. We get one shot, no rehearsals and no re-takes. If we can't see the target in the camera, we don't take the shot.

For nearly a minute Bret tried finding the deer, but couldn't. The fact the buck stood there for so long was amazing, in itself. Frustrated, I backed up and looked through the camera, trying to help Bret locate the buck. So did Jeremy. It was just terrible lighting, plain and simple, and we couldn't see the deer in the view finder.

Then the doe took off and buck followed. The only saving grace was that he was not leaving that doe. This was the only thing keeping him calm, even though he obviously saw us. This is very un-Coues deer like behavior, especially for such an old buck. The fact we'd just blown a perfect opportunity left all of us extremely frustrated. Just like that, I watched my deer slam dreams slip away. Had it not been for trying to capture this footage for TV, well, we know the outcome. Then again, were it not for TV, I wouldn't be on this hunt. In situations like this, I'm always having to remind myself to do my job and get the kill shot on film.

Given the fact the buck was sticking so tight to the doe, Jeremy suggested we try finding them again. This sort of thing just doesn't happen, for once a Coues busts you, they usually retreat into the thickest, nastiest cover around. There was so much brush for the deer to dive into, it left us feeling less than optimistic about our odds of ever relocating them. But we had to at least try.

Covering 50 yards, we came to another clearing and were stunned to find the buck standing perfectly broadside, staring right at us. Fortunately, the doe was calm enough that she felt safe holding in the brush. The fact the buck remained in the clearing, where he could better keep and eye on her, greatly helped our cause.

I wasted no time nestling the stock of the .243 into the shooting sticks and getting a steady rest. Just as I was confirming everything with Bret, my heart sank when I looked back and saw the buck take a few steps forward, then stop behind a bush. There was enough density to the foliage that it prevented my taking a shot.

The buck stood just over 200 yards away. Patiently, we waited for him to move, and eventually he did. There was only one direction he could go which would allow me to get a clear shot, and fortunately he did precisely what we needed him to. As the buck turned 180° and took one step out from behind the bush, I pulled the trigger.

Instantly the report of the bullet finding its mark hit our ears, and when Jeremy saw the buck go down, it was time for hugs and high-fives. Approaching where the deer fell, however, he was nowhere to be seen. I about lost it as I felt stomach turn. The shot felt good, and obviously looked good when the buck dropped.

Rewinding the tape, we played back the shot in slow motion. This is where having a camera is nice. The buck did go down, no question, but the shot hit him in the back leg. Obviously the buck spun and took off quicker than I thought, and I failed to compensate for this when I fired.

Scouring the area, we could see where the buck had fallen, as evidenced by the dry, red dirt and little pebbles that were cleared from a small area. We also found a large chunk of bone, no doubt a piece of femur. There was very little blood.

Now it was time to track. With a broken right hind leg, I was surprised at how quickly the deer seemed to be moving. Small, semicircular patterns in the dirt dug by the buck's toes, confirmed his leg was broken and helped to keep us on the right set of tracks.

Judas, our tracker, was invaluable along the way. When Jeremy and I lost the buck's tracks over dense rocks and thick cactus patches, Judas never skipped a beat. He was as good as any African tracker I'd hunted with.

Within an hour of hitting the buck, we ran out of daylight. Not once had the deer laid down, and only a couple times did we find where he'd stopped. Marking our last tracks, we headed back to camp. I didn't have much to say at the dinner table or around the campfire that night, and trying to sleep was a waste of time. I was disgusted with myself, for I simply hate these kinds of situations.

At sunup the next morning we were back on the track, right where we'd left off. I was hoping to hear coyotes nearby, or see flocks of buzzards gathering around a carcass, but no such luck.

Judas, my tracker on this Mexico Coues deer hunt, would hold his own against any trackers I've been with in other parts of the world.

LIFE IN THE SCOPE: THE WEST

Thus far we'd covered about 300 yards from where I hit the deer. Another 50 yards, and we found where the buck finally bedded down. He spent quite a bit of time there, but he'd only lost a small amount of blood. Right then I knew this buck wasn't dead. It takes a lot of blood loss for these animals to expire, and it wasn't going to happen with this buck. If we found him, we knew we'd need to get another bullet into him.

Then we caught a break, or so we hoped. The buck's tracks led to an expansive opening with only a small strip of brush running through the middle of it.

While Jeremy took his rifle and waited at the opposite end, I slowly continued along the track with Judas. If we found the buck I'd take the shot. If we spooked the deer, hopefully Jeremy would finish the job.

There was about 150 yards of this small, brushy strip to cover. It was barely 10 yards wide, so if the buck was in there, we were going to find him. With only 50 yards to go, my optimism faded, as I thought for sure we would have seen the buck by now.

Then Judas stopped, pointed at the ground, and drew an imaginary line connecting the deer's tracks with a brushy patch that lay ahead. It was obvious by the arching drag marks in the dirt that we were still on the buck's trail. Judas sensed the deer was just ahead.

A few more steps forward and movement beneath the brush caught my eye. It was only 50 yards from me, but too dense to lace a bullet through. There was no question it was our buck, as he moved gingerly, his back leg obviously broken.

As the deer limped away, I picked a tiny opening and fired. I heard the bullet hit the mark, entering behind the last rib and penetrating into the chest cavity. But he didn't go down. When the deer scooted out the back side of the brushline, Jeremy finished him off, putting the buck down for good.

While walking up on that heavy-racked buck, many emotions raced through my mind. I was happy, of course, but still upset with how it all unfolded. Then again, that's hunting and these things happen.

That Coues deer culminated what was a banner deer season for me, and I knew we likely would not have found that buck were it not for the exceptional tracking efforts of Judas. Simply put, this buck was the result of a total team effort.

Back at camp, Jeremy laid a tape to the buck and informed me he would have scored 114-inches had it not been for two broken tines. As it was, he measured 109-inches, one inch shy of making the Boone & Crock-

*Tagging a record book Coues deer in Sonora, Mexico surpassed
even my wildest dreams.*

ett all-time rankings, but plenty good for making their awards category. As with the other record book animals I've been fortunate to take, I didn't feel compelled to list him in the books. Knowing what he scored and all the details of the hunt, that's all I needed to store in my memory bank.

The following season I was back with Jeremy, hunting the same land in Sonora. Though mule deer were our primary target, if we happened across a big Coues deer, I wanted to try for it. We saw one nice Coues buck, walking out from behind a huge cactus patch.

I'm still kicking myself for passing up this 114" Coues deer the year after taking my buck. At least this hunter, Mark Duggen, was all smiles with my decision, for he made a perfect shot on the buck.

Looking at him through binoculars, he appeared good, but not as big as the buck I'd taken a year ago. Jeremy had another hunter in camp, Mark Duggen, who wanted a Coues deer in the worst way. Figuring this would be a good buck for him, Jeremy encouraged Mark to go try for the deer. He did, and killed it. It taped out to 114-inches. Go figure.

The only glimpse we caught of the buck when glassing was from the side, and his mass and little kickers simply eluded us. We were happy for Mark, and even happier when he decided on having a lifesize mount of this buck, allowing him to cherish his hunt for eternity.

For this part of Sonora, those were two exceptional Coues deer. They grow bigger to the north, but for Jeremy, these were the two biggest Coues bucks he'd taken in 11 years of hunting the area. Results like that made me further realize how truly dynamic these animals were, and gave me a heightened appreciation of hunting them in this harsh, yet very captivating, desert habitat.

Chapter 16:

Father-Son Pronghorns

Warm weather, prime land and lots of animals. Those are the ingredients for the ideal pronghorn hunt. This one would be especially memorable, though, for it was the first time Dad and I would hunt antelope, together.

I've been on more hunts with my Dad than anyone. After all, he's the one who introduced me to hunting and the outdoors at an early age. He's the one who had me shooting a gun by age two, catching steelhead at age four, and running a trap line at age 10.

Whatever hunting trip Dad would go on when I was small, he'd go out of his way to take me along whenever feasible. Some of my fondest childhood memories are being with him when he shot one of his biggest blacktails, and made an incredible shot on the first black bear I'd ever seen. Then there were those cold, wet days in the goose blind, where so many birds flocked into the decoys, we had to shout just to hear one another. I remember one photo we got of a honker actually plucking the corn from the very blind we sat in.

For more than 40 years I've been making outdoor memories with my dad, Jerry Haugen. But our father-son relationship goes well beyond those in the field. My dad was a high school biology teacher for more than 30 years. He was the best biology teacher I ever had – high school, college, grad-school or otherwise. He was also a coach.

For years our lives revolved around athletics. On the football team at Thurston High School, in Springfield, Oregon, where Dad taught and I graduated from, he was the quarterback coach. I was the quarterback. He also coached the defensive backs, kickers and punters. I played all three of those positions, too, gaining all-league honors at three positions, all-state honors in two.

Dad was also the head basketball coach for several years. I played point guard for him one year, the season we went to state for the first time in years. He also helped on the golf team, which I also competed on. We went to state my senior year, the first time in school history. Dad helped me in track and field, where I became one of the nation's leading freshman javelin throwers. A severe shoulder injury ended that career, but it was a blast while it lasted.

It's fair to say that I've shared more special moments with my dad, be it in the field or through athletics, than anyone else on earth. We've shared tears of joy and tears of sorrow. We've endured much together, and my mom, Jean Haugen, has always been supportive of our close relationship and adventures.

I had the perfect childhood. As an only child with parents who always got along and have now been married nearly 50 years, our family focus was always on doing things together. Today, my parents live 52 yards from me and my family, that's the reading I get on my rangefinder.

In all honesty, the job I have of hosting television shows, writing and speaking is not an easy one. Long hours and many days away from home make it tough on my family. One fall, we started filming shows on August 5th and wrapped up the season on December 12th. During those months I was home a total of five days. Prior to that I spent a couple months hunting in Africa, New Zealand and around the West during the spring and summer months, and that all came on the heels of two straight months of attending sportshows and delivering seminars.

With such a hectic schedule, I need help, and Dad is always there for me and the family – so is Mom. From mowing the lawn to fixing anything and everything, from taking me to the airport in the wee hours of the morning to driving me to the next hunt so I can work on the computer to meet magazine article deadlines, Dad is always more than willing to help out. My wife quit giving the honey-do lists to me years ago, now she just hands them directly to Dad.

Simply put, Dad is the greatest man I've ever met. I've never heard him swear, and only seen him get mad one time, during a tense basketball practice. He's the most patient man I know, and goes out of his way to always talk with and listen to others. He's the kind of man I still strive to be like. Even at my age, I'm still learning from my dad.

One of the greatest challenges of my job is accepting how much time it takes away from my family, including the time I used to spend with Dad. We aren't able to go on as many hunts as we used to, but we still make it a point of getting out together when we can. It's never enough.

One hunt we'd never shared the joys of was that for pronghorns. Dad had taken some nice bucks in Oregon and Wyoming, as I had in other states, but we'd never been on an antelope hunt, together. Finally, in 2007, we had the opportunity.

Guy and Shanna Howell, of Center of The Nation Outfitters in Colony, Wyoming, invited both Dad and I to come hunt antelope with them. A year prior I'd hunted pronghorns with them, alone, and also took that awesome double drop tine buck featured in Chapter 8. Going into this hunt, I knew exactly what to expect.

I'd spent a great deal of time on the Howell's land, and knew it well. In the spring of this same year, I had my family out there hunting turkeys, prairie dogs and riding horses. I love being with the Howell family and reveling in their glorious land.

Knowing Dad and I hadn't had the chance to hunt together much in recent years, Guy handed me the keys to his rig on the first morning of the hunt. "You know where to go and how to hunt, you don't need me," Guy smiled. "You and your dad go out and just have fun, together." That's the kind of people the Howell's are.

On a spring turkey hunt, the family was able to join me on the Howell's ranch.
Our sons were with Tiffany and I when we took two nice Merriam's.

Enjoying a glowing sunrise, Dad and I looked at buck after buck. Sipping on hot cocoa, it was a relaxing time. From one vantage point, we could see three shooter bucks that got Dad's attention, all in different directions. The first buck we put the move on didn't have the cutters we'd hoped for. The second buck was one we wanted, but he chased a group of does off the property line by the time we reached him.

It was mid-September and the pronghorn rut was lingering on. It made for easy spotting, and easy stalking as long as we played it smart.

On the third buck we closed in on, we couldn't get close enough to get the shot on film. Rather than push that buck, we figured we'd return later in the day to see where he was at, if need be.

Over the course of the next few hours we glassed hundreds of head of antelope on the Howells' 40,000 acres of real estate. Then we found a buck that really got Dad excited. He was heavy with average length. It was the mass that Dad liked. In this, the furthest northeastern corner of Wyoming you can get in, there aren't many record-class pronghorns. There's the odd one here and there, but this is more a place that if you see an animal that's a good representative of the species, you take him. These kind of bucks are seen all day long, so it comes down to which one appeals to you.

The buck was with more than 20 does, and he was chasing one of them extra hard. Then another smaller buck encroached, and Dad's buck didn't like that. The bigger buck chased him, fought and ran him a half-mile away from the harem. By the time the buck returned, another lesser buck was after his does.

All this action was taking place in a big, open, yellow grass field. A gentle ridge overlooking the flat, extended well over a mile, meaning every buck up there could see what was going on. Vast, open land to the east and west of the animals allowed more curious bucks to see what was happening. The only place there were no other animals was to the south, and that's where Dad's stalk would commence.

This wasn't a drive up and shoot 'em sorta hunt, it was the real deal. Dad's stalk began over a mile from where his buck was. Initially using the tree line for cover, we then relied on 100 or so yards of cattails to get us to a ditch line. Once in the ditch, we followed it for nearly 800 yards, then had it made.

The final 40 yards of the ditch line shallowed up, meaning we had to belly-crawl the rest of the way. Once we broke over the burm, Dad's buck was right where we'd last seen him, along with five other bucks which had moved in.

During the 45 minutes we had into this stalk, curious bucks came from everywhere to see what the activity was all about. Pronghorns are a gregarious animal, and when the rut's waning and only the odd doe comes in to heat, all the bucks seem to know about it. That's exactly what was happening here.

For the better part of a half-hour, Dad tried getting a shot, but his buck just wouldn't stand still. It was either chasing bucks, fighting bucks, or dogging a doe. All the rest of the does were balled-up, not moving. The camera man, Sam Potter, was all set. We just needed a window for Dad to shoot.

Finally, the wad of does started breaking up and moving to the left. The doe in heat was with them. Now there was some distance being created between the bucks on the perimeter and the does. Once Dad's buck started chasing competing bucks away, then returning to the herd, we knew his chance at a shot was coming.

The third time the big buck left the herd of does and chased a buck, he returned slowly to the harem. He even paused to chew on some grass. "What's the distance?" Dad asked. Struggling to get a reading through the tall grass, it finally registered 263 yards on my rangefinder.

With the Trijicon scope turned to the highest power, Dad took a firm rest, slowed his breathing and pressured the trigger. As usual, he connected with a perfect shot, this one to the heart. That's one thing, I know I can always count on Dad come crunch time. I can count on one hand the number of times I've seen Dad miss in the past 40 years. The buck went a short distance and collapsed. It was a fitting end to one of the most enjoyable pronghorn stalks I'd ever been a part of, and the fact it was with Dad made it that much sweeter.

We could have gone out and got my buck that afternoon, but instead we took our time. We didn't want the hunt to end so soon. We drove around looking at animals, and spent some time with the Howell's, watching all the girls ride horses as soon as they got home from school. The Howell's have four daughters, all of whom rodeo, competitively.

Then we returned to our cozy little cabin. Here we sat and talked in the comfort of lawn chairs. We had the spotting scope with us so we could watch antelope milling about. This continued for a few hours, until darkness fell.

The next morning Guy would join us, for there was one specific buck I wanted to find and Guy knew where he was at. The buck was a non-

112   LIFE IN THE SCOPE: THE WEST

My dad, Jerry Haugen, with the first of two pronghorns we took on this memorable father-son hunt.

typical with a right horn that protruded 90° out his head. There was a trophy buck that Guy had seen in early August, one he figured was well over 16-inches tall, but he hadn't seen him for a few weeks. That made the decision easy, as I have a thing about pursing nontypical animals.

We drove to the back part of Howell's property, where the freak buck had last been seen. From where we glassed, the Montana border was within shooting range to the north, as was the South Dakota border to the east. The second herd we spotted had our buck in it.

The hard part was going to be getting close enough for a shot. There was no cover, no undulating ground, and over 60 sets of eyes in the herd. We had no choice but to wait. Two hours later the herd started moving, and the buck was bringing up the rear.

They were heading up one coulee, so we headed up another. Some 600 yards ahead the two coulees would meet, and if we timed it right, we could get in shooting position and just wait for the animals to walk right by. It sounded good, in theory, but didn't pan out. Busting us, the whole herd took off and our buck was with them.

We watched them run for over a mile, then our buck started separating from the herd. While the herd continued running over a distant hill, our buck peeled off into a protected bowl, then, an hour later, he bedded down. We all looked at each other and grinned.

It took more than an hour to reach the buck, and fortunately he hadn't moved. He was still all alone, bedded against the backside of the bowl in an effort to escape the 30 mile per hour winds. The sage brush in which he laid was tall, but at least we could see his horns. We'd have to wait for him to stand in order to get a shot.

After more than two hours of patiently waiting, the buck finally arose, stretched and started walking our direction. He had no clue we were there. From 250 yards, the buck closed to within 200 yards, then 150. Laying prone, the .270 securely rested on my pack. The buck started slowly walking to our right. He wasn't going to get any closer.

The moment the buck stopped, I put the tip of the AccuPoint on the line where brown fur met white fur, behind his shoulder. At first I thought I missed, seeing dirt fly from behind the buck. Then I saw a red spot appear and the buck tipped over. The 130 grain bullet had passed clean through.

He was the most unique pronghorn I'd ever taken. Heck, he was one of the most unique big game animals I'd ever taken. A stout, mature buck with heavy, black headgear and a deformed right horn that stood out from a mile away, he was simply awesome. I was so pleased that Dad was with me during the entire seven hours we spent in pursuit of this buck.

Our father-son antelope adventure was over. Success on this hunt came easy for both of us. That's one of the joys of open-country pronghorn hunting, there are few stresses given the number of animals continually being seen. If you can shoot straight, you know filling a tag on such hunts is only a matter of time.

I love targeting nontypical animals, and the fact my good friend, outfitter Guy Howell, and Dad were by my side on this hunt, carried extra special meanings for me.

A few months following the pronghorn hunt with my dad, I returned to Wyoming and took this dandy 10-point whitetail. I never tire of hunting this magical land.

But this hunt was more than just about filling tags. It was a time for Dad and I to reflect on the 40 years of hunting experiences we'd been so fortunate to share with one another. It was about creating more memories and rekindling bonds. It was about spending quality time together.

This hunt would not have happened were it not for the generosity of the Howells, and to them we will always be grateful. We ended up getting some good pronghorn action on film, and everyone was pleased. A couple months later I returned to the Howells, alone, to hunt whitetails. It was the end of the rut, but there were still plenty of impressive bucks moving around.

On the second morning of that whitetail hunt I took a nice 10-pointer on film for the Outdoor America television show. In fact, all three of those hunts with the Howell's aired on the same program.

From where my whitetail buck fell, I could look across the valley and see where Dad had taken his pronghorn buck. Though Dad wasn't by my side on this deer hunt, I knew that he was with me in prayer and in spirit, just as he is on all my hunts, and how he always will be.

Chapter 17:

Mule Deer Duo

Because I'd already lost three days on this Montana mule deer hunt, I almost cancelled it. With only two days to hunt, I didn't feel there was enough time to find a big buck. I was wrong.

Coming off an elk hunt in Wyoming, I wasn't sure we'd have enough time to head up to Montana and try for mule deer. The elk hunt lasted four days longer than anticipated, and I had to be in another state to film another deer hunt in three days.

I called Harold Gilchrist in Montana, owner of Landers Fork Outfitters, whose land we'd be hunting on, and he felt confident we could get it done in two days. Tight timelines, travel, budgets, obligations to outfitters...these are some of the things we take into constant consideration when filming hunts for outdoor television.

Given the fact we already had our tag in-hand, and that we were only about a six hour drive from the Montana mule deer grounds, we decided to give it a try. I knew there were some big bucks in this area, and didn't want to regret at least not giving it a whirl.

Travis Ralls, my main man on the camera, and I rolled into camp with only a few minutes of daylight remaining. It was enough time to have Harold drive us around some of the property we'd be hunting, so we'd know what to expect come morning.

At first light we were seeing deer right from camp. Lots of deer. There were so many deer, in fact, we couldn't leave camp until daylight, for a shooter buck could be just about anywhere. There had been a few big bucks hanging in two nearby drainages, so we checked those places out first. We were hunting in the Marias River Breaks, northwest of the little town of Loma, Montana. It was the middle of November.

The country is deceiving. When we first arrived, the land appeared flat as could be. Then, the closer we drove toward the river, the more the topography changed. From vast grain fields to rugged breaks to a meandering river, there was a big shift in habitat, and I now understood why there were so many deer in the area.

When I first chatted with Harold about hunting this land, he said we could expect to see over 200 deer a day. That was a conservative estimate, for we saw that many muleys by noon. Though we were seeing some good bucks, we couldn't find the big buck's Harold knew were in the area.

All morning we watched bucks. Some were chasing does, some were feeding, some were bedding on south facing slopes in an attempt to warm their bodies in the cold temperatures. Nighttime temperatures plummeted to below zero, and things were in no hurry to warm up once the sun had risen. Still, there was no shortage of deer to look at.

We did see one dandy 4x4 that I would have liked to have had. He carried a heavy rack, no more than 24-inches wide, but dark and massive. We simply couldn't catch up to him as he dogged does from canyon to canyon. It's amazing how much land rutting bucks can cover.

After a quick bite to eat we were back to glassing early in the afternoon. Clouds had now moved in and temperatures began to warm. Figuring the deer would start moving earlier than they had been, we wasted no time hitting key glassing points. By 2:00 p.m. deer were coming out of the breaks to graze in the surrounding grass fields. By 3:00, it was as if the flood gates had been opened. Deer were everywhere. By 3:30 we'd seen well over 400 deer that day. Some very nice bucks were out there, but the ones we wanted either moved off before we could reach them, or were too far in the distance to go after.

After not finding a buck we wanted on the upper flats, we headed down through the breaks, to check out the alfalfa fields along the eastern banks of the Marias River. In the far, southeast corner of the field stood five does and a dandy buck. The does contentedly fed while the buck hopped from one to another, sniffing to see which one was in heat.

The buck didn't travel far from the protection of the rugged ravines he'd been spending his days in. As more does fed out from the breaks, the buck checked them as they walked by. A quick glance through the spotting scope, and there was no second-guessing on this buck.

We had to act fast, for if the buck hooked up with a hot doe and followed her into the middle of the field, we'd likely be dealing with too many eyes to move in for a good shot. The field was expansive, several hundred yards across. From where we were there was too much open ground between us and the buck, so we had to hoof it back up into the breaks and begin our stalk from above.

Using the jagged hills and deep ravines for cover, Travis and I made good time. We had to run most of the 1/2 mile, not because filming light was fading, but because the buck was out of sight and we didn't want to lose track of him.

Legs rubbery from the run and lungs stinging from the cold air, we slowly crept up to the last little hillside, trying to catch our breath. Our buck was in the same place, still inspecting does.

We had no choice but to slowly creep along the bottom of where the gumbo hill met the valley floor, hoping to remain hidden. There was no vegetation to conceal us, so we moved slowly and hoped our camouflage performed. Halfway through our maneuver, a small herd of does came out of the exact ravine we'd hoped to get to for a shot. They busted us, snorted, and ran back into the breaks.

This alerted the does our buck was with, and they also retreated back into the hills. With our buck following close behind, he had no clue as to what spooked the does. Rushing to get set, the shot was going to have to happen in the next few seconds or the buck would be gone.

Travis quickly got his tripod on solid, level ground, the camera turned to full magnification. I rapidly ranged the buck and got a reading just over 360 yards. Not ideal TV range, but it would have to do. Anchoring the .30 T/C in the V of the shooting sticks, I tracked the buck in my Trijicon scope as he moved higher and higher up the hillside. Then he stopped and looked back over his left shoulder, quartering away.

At the shot, the reverberation echoed off the surrounding canyon walls, then the bullet found it's mark with a solid thud. We could see the impact of the bullet before we could hear it. Both were good signs. The buck stumbled down the hill and stopped, still on his feet. He was definitely hurting, but not wanting to leave anything to chance, I hit him again. This time he went down for good.

The buck's rack spanned into the mid-20-inch range, about average for a mature mule deer in this area. Not the widest buck around, but it was his deep forks, tall tines and amazing symmetry that made me want this mule deer. He was the most symmetrical muley I'd taken, and to me, these qualities made him something beyond just your average mule deer. The fact we pulled it off in one day was even more remarkable.

The next morning we awoke to four inches of snow on the ground, and crisp, cold air. Rather than risk heading home on icy roads, we chose to tag along with Mel Morris, one of Harold's clients. I'd met Mel the previous September, in Harold's elk camp east of Great Falls. We were both bowhunting then, on a place where never before had I seen so many big bulls. We talked about maybe connecting during the November rifle season with Harold, and it worked out.

Montana's Marias River Breaks holds some dandy mule deer. This is the most symmetrical 4x4 I'd ever taken.

We had about three hours to spend before Travis and I had to hit the road and get to our next hunt, a conservative 18 hour drive given the poor road conditions we'd encounter along the way. We headed east of where I got my buck, to the famed Missouri River.

Our intent was to intercept deer as they fed from the hay fields along the river, up into the Missouri River Breaks. Our plan worked. The first spot we stopped to glass from, we saw over 30 deer, 12 of which were bucks, one of which was a handsome 4x4. He was the buck Mel wanted.

Before making our move, we had to let the deer work deeper into the draw about 400 yards, where broken country would allow us to commence stalking. The deer were well over a half-mile in the distance, but seemed much closer, their dark bodies standing out in sharp contrast to the fresh, ivory snow.

Once the deer worked into the hills, we had to circle down the ridge and follow their tracks. They were moving into the wind, and we had to take the same route. Now our biggest concern was catching up with them before the does started spreading out and bedding down.

Poking our heads up over a small saddle, we found Mel's buck. As we inched closer to reach a solid shooting position, we nearly came face to face with a half dozen other deer. They'd moved in between us and Mel's buck, and we hadn't seen them until now. Fortunately they didn't detect us, so remained calm. Unfortunately, we had no shot from that position.

Backing off the hill, we had to give those deer time to move out of the way. We waited nearly 45 minutes, then all was clear. Mel's buck was nowhere in sight, but we felt confident he'd be with does in the next bowl over. Quietly we edged up to the back side of the bowl, looked over it's rim and saw nothing. Not a deer. Our hearts sank.

"He's got to be over in that next little pocket," Mel pointed out. We all agreed. From where we stood, we could see several deer in the bottom of the ravine and on adjacent hillsides, but none were Mel's buck.

Working up and over the edge of the next rim, we found two bucks on the far side. They were half-heartedly sparring and didn't see us. Closer we edged, seeing more deer with each advancing step. Before long we had seven does and five bucks within 100 yards of us, but no big buck.

At this point we were too close to exchange words, for fear of spooking any deer. But we were all thinking the same thing. Either the buck had made it around the next ridge, or he was right below us. Feeling there was no way Mel's deer could have made it into the next draw without our seeing him, we slowly continued crawling forward in intense anticipation. I had the shooting sticks ready to go, Travis was rolling tape, Harold was keeping an eye out and Mel was ready to shoot.

Mel had done quite a bit of hunting in his life, but this experience was different. When filming hunts for TV shows, the aspects of the sport change. Many pressures are placed on the shoulders of the shooter that have never been felt before. On several occasions we've tried filming other hunters in camp, and rarely does it work out as smoothly as everyone hopes.

On a pronghorn hunt one year, a seasoned, worldly hunter missed three record book bucks on film, all inside 100 yards. On a deer hunt, we had another experienced hunter shoot clean over the back of a big buck, killing a smaller buck behind. On an archery elk hunt, a guy who had killed way more elk than me, missed three big bulls inside 30 yards – all clean misses. Every one of those hunters who missed related their feelings to me, and all shared a common thread of how much pressure they felt knowing their hunt was going to be on TV. I was praying Mel wasn't feeling the same way right at this moment.

Inching forward, two does popped into view. Then the shape of a high, dark rack transformed before us. It was Mel's buck, and he was 70 yards away. The shooting sticks likely weren't necessary at this range, but again, not having seen Mel in this type of pressure situation, I slowly erected them. Travis was already on the deer, and Mel slipped the .30 T/C into position.

Just as Mel got ready to take the shot, a doe stepped in behind the buck. She then moved slightly up the hill, but was still behind him. Mel was wanting to

Mel Morris (left), teamed up with Harold Gilchrist to score on this handsome Montana mule deer. Capturing this hunt on film was a big bonus, and was the highlight of the entire show.

shoot in the worst way, but Travis called it off, fearing the bullet could hit bone, fragment and potentially cripple the doe. The odds of that happening were slim, but possible, and had that occurred, a perfectly good situation would have gone awry. This is where having a camera man with a cool head is invaluable.

The buck had not seen us, and was so pumped full of testosterone, I don't think he would have taken off had he known we were there. He was focused on a hot doe and that's all he cared about.

For more than 30 seconds – an eternity at this short range, under these pressures – we waited. Mel was getting antsy. It's hard, holding off on such a big buck, but for TV, everything has to be just right or all the efforts are for not.

Finally, the doe took another couple steps forward, clearing from behind the buck. Travis gave Mel the green light and he wasted no time squeezing the trigger. You couldn't have walked up and placed the bullet any more precisely in the bullseye than where Mel's shot hit. Taking out both lungs, the snow faded to crimson on the opposite side of the buck. The deer made a death run right toward us and collapsed.

Mel was elated, for he'd just taken the biggest mule deer of his life. I was elated with how calm Mel remained under pressure. What more could two hunters ask for? Two handsome four points in two days, and both experiences captured on film whereby allowing the memories to be vividly relived for a lifetime.

Chapter 18:

The First Bugle

There comes a time for every young hunter
to enter into the elk woods. The toughest part as a parent
can be picking the right time.

Perched atop a grassy knoll, the setting sun soothed our cold bodies. Peering through binoculars and spotting scopes, guide, Aaron Hensen, myself and my eight year old son, Braxton, all eagerly searched for elk.

Braxton's job was to look at distant tree lines for elk emerging to feed. He was doing great, then he heard a cry. We all heard it; a clear, high-pitched squeal emanating from the canyon below.

"What was that?" whispered Braxton, eager to hear what animal would make such a sound. Again, the sound shot up the ridge, this time even more clear. It was too brushy to see what was making the sound, but Aaron and I both felt it was a cat, either a bobcat or young cougar.

Then Aaron spotted a herd of elk feeding into a clearing. Quickly we turned all optics their way. For Braxton, it was the first time he'd watched elk through a spotting scope.

"Wow, they look so close," he exclaimed, right eye glued to the eye piece. "Is there a big enough bull in there?" he followed.

Closer inspection by both Aaron and I confirmed that there was a good bull in the herd, just not quite the caliber we were looking for. It's a good thing, too, for given their location, there's no way we could have reached them by nightfall.

"Nope," I whispered to Braxton. "But can you count his points?" The bull was moving, and not easy to follow in the scope. It would have been simple for me to take the scope, reposition and focus it for Braxton, but he needed to learn how to use this hunting tool.

It took him a while, and with a little guidance, he got it. He reset the scope, cranked down the power and refocused it to his eye. Then he began counting points. "Six," he exclaimed. "Look close at both sides," I encouraged.

"Oh, he has five points on one side," Braxton noticed. "He's not big enough to shoot?"

It was early in our Idaho hunt, atop the stunning setting of the Joseph Plains, and I explained to Braxton that though this was a mature bull, we were looking for something bigger. With less than an hour of daylight remaining, we loaded into the ATV and headed down a logging road, to another glassing locale.

Getting youngsters into the field and educating them on animal behavior is important to building solid hunting skills. Here, Braxton and I study an elk rub, one of many such moments we shared during this hunt.

As we neared a switchback, a female cougar leaped from the brush in front of us, pranced down the road, then disappeared into a dense wall of brush. "Did you see that!" Braxton yelled, his excitement impossible to keep bottled. The cat moved down toward the crying sounds we'd heard earlier, likely her offspring of the year.

In a short time Braxton had seen several head of elk, mule deer, whitetails and something many outdoorsmen go a lifetime without seeing, a mountain lion. His introduction into the elk woods couldn't have been scripted out any better.

That night Braxton had some unique stories to share with other hunters back at camp. The fact he was excited and wanting to share, pleased me to no end. Even better was the undivided attention given to him by the more than a dozen adults in camp. All of these men were seasoned elk hunters. They were also good people to know when to listen to a youngster, then encourage that future hunter.

We slept well that night, arising at 4:00 the next morning to do it all over again. This day started different, however. Heavy clouds and high winds replaced the clear skies we'd had the evening prior. Six inches of fresh snow also blanketed the ground.

"Do you still want to go out?" I offered Braxton, not wanting to force him into an uncomfortable situation. "Da-ad, it's snowing...helloooo, of course I want to go!" We don't get much snow where we live in Oregon's Willamette Valley.

I didn't tell him that the thermometer registered 18°. I just made sure he was bundled up and was ready to walk. Giving him a pair of hand warmers made warding off the cold easier.

Piling into the ATV, Aaron drove us down an old logging road. Then we walked. It wasn't a hard walk, in fact, it kept our bodies warm and Braxton enjoyed the snow. With a half-mile behind us, we crested a balled knob only to be met with high winds and intense, driving snow.

Winds gusted up to 25 miles per hour, taking the windchill to well below zero. I was worried. It was the coldest temperatures Braxton had ever been in, but he didn't say a word.

Gathering behind the base of a fat pine tree, we hunkered together to stay warm. From there we glassed for elk on adjacent hillsides, where we found a few cows and some small bulls. Braxton got to watch them feed and interact through binoculars.

Over the next hour we watched two different herds from that spot. Then we started getting cold; it was time to move on. We walked more than three miles that morning, through incessant snow that was now knee-deep to Braxton. He didn't complain once.

Aaron, being the top-notch guide he is, continually encouraged Braxton. He asked if he needed help. He'd walk ahead, hide behind a tree, then toss snowballs at him. He made it fun, and most importantly, he left Braxton wanting more.

At one point, a steep grade lay before us. "Braxton, do you want me to carry you up that thing?" smiled Aaron. Braxton declined. It was a pride thing.

In his fun way, Aaron ran at Braxton, picked him up, tossed him over his shoulder and ran 50 yards up the steep hillside.

When I caught up with them, Aaron looked at me and smiled, "There's tall grass laying under that snow, and quite a bit of mud. It could have been frustrating for Braxton trying to make it up that thing." He was exactly right.

That thoughtfulness on Aaron's part was one of the most kind, potentially pivotal moments of the hunt. Had Braxton struggled up that hill, gotten all hot and sweaty, then cold and frustrated, there's no telling how that could have impacted him. That kind of generosity, effort and awareness is what builds hunters, and what separates top guides and mentors from average ones.

We hunted hard all morning long, and Braxton didn't miss a beat. Showing him how to read elk sign in fresh snow, observe how animals feed into the wind, and examining food sources and rubs made during the rut surpassed any lesson he'd receive from his third grade science class.

After a hot lunch back at camp, I expected Braxton to hang inside by the fire. Instead, he played outside in the snow.

By mid-afternoon the snow had melted, and we enjoyed a stunning sunset as we watched a nice mule deer buck acting rutty with a herd of does. The next morning was cold and clear, but Braxton was ready to get after it.

The lack of snow made for favorable walking, especially on the steep, downhill climbs we faced. By daylight we reached our first glassing point, and getting there wasn't easy. Again, Aaron chose the path of least resistance, for Braxton's sake. His forethought paid off.

Not only did Braxton make it to the rocky outcropping from which we'd glass for the next couple of hours, but he spotted elk all by himself. To use a spotting scope, grid the land and spot elk before adults is a huge confidence builder for a growing hunter. Of course, it's up to the mentor to create such a situation and facilitate the learning which fosters developing minds, whereby allowing a common goal to be achieved. Aaron and I strived to do exactly that with Braxton.

Watching elk from a distance and discussing their natural behavior was a thrill for Braxton. With no shooter bulls worth going after, we hiked out of the area, not an easy task.

"I'm thinking we should head to the Bull Hole this afternoon," piped Aaron. In his tone I could sense he really was asking me, "do you think Braxton can make it?"

I'd been in the Bull Hole on a previous hunt with Boulder Creek Outfitters, and shot a bear down in there. I knew it was very rugged land, but that it held big bulls, and lots of them.

Figuring we'd get a bull and that we could head out the bottom, I chose to go for it. Braxton agreed.

Hiking down into the Bull Hole, the going was straight forward: lots of downhill traversing with dense, brushy spots. Braxton did good, but I prayed he wouldn't have to walk out the same way we went in.

One of my primary goals on this hunt was to call in a bull for Braxton. But the temperatures were into the low 'teens at night, and barely into the 40s during most days. The elk were also establishing their winter herds. Still, it was only mid-October and both Aaron and I felt confident we could call in a bull.

Setting up on a point overlooking a vast valley, we watched several herds of elk feeding in distant meadows. They were unapproachable. Then we cow called. When three bulls answered back from down in the Bull Hole, Braxton smiled, "That's just like the sounds you make at home all the time" He'd heard his first bugle.

Then we saw a lone bull, well over 1,000 yards away, chasing a single cow across a ridgeline. I called, he stopped. I called again, he bugled. A third cow call got him excited. He bugled, left his cow and barreled downhill on the run.

It took the bull 20 minutes to close the distance and he bugled at every sound we made, over 30 times in all. Braxton even blew a few notes on the open-reed call, and got the bull to respond as it moved through the rugged Bull Hole. Talk about rewarding.

When the bull bugled at 10 yards, the look on Braxton's face was priceless. When the bull emerged from heavy brush and stood broadside at eight yards, Braxton's eyes grew even larger. Then the bull winded us and took off.

"Why didn't you shoot?" Braxton pleaded. I explained that he was not an old bull, only a small 5x6 that had a few years to grow. That was one of the hardest animals I'd ever passed, as I so wanted Braxton to be there when we got a bull down. It was the right thing to do and an ideal time for Braxton to learn about decisions hunters are faced with.

Another test came when we had to hike back out of the Bull Hole in the dark. Braxton refused help, and though it took us a while to crawl up that steep ridge, we made it out, two hours after dark. The sense of accomplishment Braxton received from this single outing is what shapes character. It's what instills work ethics, forms relationships and defines the parameters of our hunting culture. It makes elk hunters.

The next morning came early, and understandably, Braxton was tired and too sore to head out. Not wanting to push him and risk a negative experience, I let him rest. "I'll go out with you in the afternoon," promised Braxton as he drifted back to sleep. Unfortunately, that's the morning I filled my tag.

Never have I been so proud of Braxton than when he overcame both physical and mental challenges to get himself in and out of the Bull Hole. From where we're sitting here, we called a 5x6 bull to within eight yards. He bugled over 30 times.

128

*The culmination of our concerted efforts resulted in this
nice Idaho bull.*

"Hey, let's go get Braxton so he can see what this part is all about," offered Aaron. Again, his thoughtfulness shined through. True, it took time, but time is what's so precious, what we need more of in raising today's future hunters.

Braxton was amazed by the size of a bull once on the ground. It wasn't the biggest bull we saw, but he was a good representative. Braxton helped in the quartering, skinning and caping, like he'd done on other big game, but never elk. Once we got the meat home, the entire family took part in the butchering and packaging festivities.

We, like many hunting families, depend almost exclusively on wild game. It's the way we choose to live, both for the gratification it offers and the optimal nutrition it provides.

Braxton's first elk hunt was about more than putting meat in the freezer. It was about forming bonds, shaping character, learning responsibility and pushing his physical and mental limits to achieve goals. When Braxton heard that first bugle, it changed his life. That's what elk hunting is about.

Chapter 19:

Saskatchewan Smokepole Buck

Saskatchewan is a place I never thought I'd have the good fortune to hunt, then TV came along. On this hunt, however, technical difficulties nearly cost us.

The phone rang early one September morning, 2003. It was my producer, Steve Gruber, asking if I'd like to go to Saskatoon, Saskatchewan and try filming a whitetail hunt. I'll be the first to admit that though I'm not much of a whitetail nut, when Saskatchewan and whitetail deer are mentioned in the same sentence, it gets my attention.

In a few week's time, mid-October to be exact, I'd find myself in Saskatchewan, muzzleloader in hand, searching for one of the province's trophy bucks. In the crisp, cool darkness of the first morning, I walked a quarter mile of fenceline to reach a timbered edge by first light. Hoping to catch a good buck in the field they'd been feeding in at night, only a couple dozen does and a few smaller bucks lingered. While a 135 class buck grazed contentedly, he wasn't worth pulling the trigger on, not in Saskatchewan. We got some good footage of that buck, then decided to move on.

Checking out another area, movement along the fenceline caught my attention. A closer look through binoculars revealed two nice bucks coming down the precise path the camera man and I had walked along only minutes prior. For more than 500 yards each of their strides fell in our footsteps as they continued making their way directly toward us.

Diving into the corner of a brush-choked fence, my camera man, one of Wolf Creek Production's fill-ins, got the tripod in place and started rolling tape. I continued glassing the bucks, trying to estimate their antler size. The deer had no idea we were there. By chance we were fortunate enough to be in their path of travel as they returned from their nocturnal feeding grounds to their place of sanctuary for the day. An expansive, lowland forest lay at our back, and the bucks had to pass right by us to get there.

Safety off, I readied the muzzleloader for what would have been a simple shot. Then another buck emerged from a grove of thick brush to our left, intent on making his way to the woods where the two bucks were heading. At 400 yards the lone buck's antlers stood long and tall above his head. Prancing across a meadow to reach cover, he closed the distance to 250 yards, well out of muzzleloader range.

Without question, this was the biggest whitetail I'd ever seen. Long tines with a main frame extending beyond his white muzzle, he'd measure all of 190-inches, likely closer to 200, maybe more. His behemoth body resembled more that of an elk than any deer I'd laid eyes on.

Glancing back at the two bucks approaching down the fenceline, they were now within range. Closer they continued to come, then cut the corner at 60 yards, offering the perfect broadside shot. The smaller of the bucks would have stretched the tape to over 20 inches with his wide rack, but his lack of high tines shifted my focus to his companion.

Putting the crosshairs on the shoulder of the larger buck, his 140-inch class frame tempted me. But the vision of the leviathan I'd seen seconds prior loomed heavy in my mind. It was early in my seven day hunt, and knowing where the giant buck lived, I wasn't convinced I needed to fill my tag just yet.

"I'm on him," whispered the camera man. In other words, he wanted me to take the bigger of the two bucks. It wasn't an easy decision to make, and several thoughts raced through my mind in a fraction of a second. First there was the time factor. Though I did have seven days to hunt, three days from now, Steve Gruber would be flying in to hunt this place, and with only one camera man to share between the two of us, it would have been nice to get one kill under our belts. Then there was the size factor. Though this buck was not small by any means, he was nowhere near the monster buck we'd just seen seconds earlier. Finally, I'd not yet gotten to see a fraction of the land we were hunting, and who knows what other caliber of bucks were out there.

Processing all of this information in a split second wasn't easy, but I decided to hold off. Right then the two bucks busted us, bounded across the field, hopped the fence and disappeared into the forest. Though the camera man wasn't too thrilled, I felt confident about the decision.

Some of the bucks taken from this land over the years grace the bunkhouse walls where we were staying, showing the true potential of the region. A 26 point nontypical scoring over 270-inches first caught my eye. The 17 point 190 buck, and several 160 and greater bucks kept me gawking, hopeful that the next monster buck taken would be mine.

A handful of bucks taken from the very land I hunted in Saskatchewan.
Knowing bucks of this caliber are looming in the forest makes it hard pulling the
trigger on lesser deer.

All foreigners hunting big game in Canada must have a guide, and on this hunt I was with Elliot Maduck. At the time, Maduck had access to more than 430 square miles of private agricultural land. In addition, he had an exclusive government lease on 126 square miles of forest land. With so much land, it's no wonder much of it hadn't been hunted. It was obvious I'd only get to cover a fraction of it, so had to choose the spots wisely.

This early in the season the bucks were still hanging in bachelor groups. While some bucks displayed pre-rut behaviors, the majority were intent on amassing weight for the winter. Knowing this, we focused our efforts on locating bucks, not does.

With nightly temperatures dipping into the 'teens, there were some days the mercury popped above 80°. When the conditions are this warm, the big bucks sit tight in the brush during the day, but as the late afternoon temperatures rapidly decline, the deer can become active fairly early.

We hit it perfect, cool mornings and late afternoons, combined with a waning moon phase encouraged deer to be on the move. With each passing sunset, deer emerged from the woods earlier and earlier, setting the stage for a decisive outcome.

Over the course of the next few days, we hammered the territory hard where we'd seen the monster buck on opening morning. We never saw him again. But we did see lots of other bucks. Several of the deer we saw were 130-140 class bucks. But it was the five 170-200 point bucks I laid eyes on that kept me holding out for a big buck.

There was no question the camera man was a little miffed at me. I'd passed up multiple deer every morning on spot-and-stalk missions, and numerous bucks we watched from tree stands during evening hunts.

When Gruber rolled in to camp around 9:00 a.m. on the fourth day of my hunt, I was prepared to take a lashing for passing on so many bucks. We sat down to review the footage of the bucks I'd been passing up, including two nice bucks that morning. When the camera man finished rewinding the tape, then hit the "play" button, the screen was blank. Nothing. Nervously, he ejected that tape and inserted another that we'd filled with buck footage. Nothing on that tape either.

We went through three hours of tape we'd accumulated up to this point, and only garbled footage of a buck here and there appeared. None of the footage was usable. This is one of those times when filming TV shows for a living makes you question whether you're in the right line of work.

Here we were in one of Canada's top whitetail grounds, and we didn't have a second of footage to show for nearly four days of work. The outfitter wasn't pleased, for he was giving us this expensive hunt in return for a TV show, which would bring him business. The production company also had some money invested in this project.

At this point, there's nothing to do but stay positive and start over. The camera had simply quit recording and none of the warning signals that should have alerted us to such malfunctions engaged.

Without hesitation, Gruber and the camera man hopped in the rental car and headed to town to find a new video camera. "If I'm not back by the evening hunt, don't wait for me," he offered. "If a big buck comes in, shoot him and we'll film a recovery."

It was a long drive to town, so I knew I'd be hunting alone that evening. It was odd, hunting by myself after having a camera man attached to my hip the whole time.

Perched in a tree stand by 3:00 p.m., it didn't take long for two small bucks to wander by. By 4:15, five bucks had worked by the stand. The air was cool, the shadows from the trees grew long, and bucks were moving early. My gut feeling told me something big was going to happen.

By 5:00 p.m. smaller bucks and does raced to the edges of the crop fields along which I sat, and the fact I had a 125 and 135 class buck feeding below me made it be known to other deer in the vicinity that all was safe.

For two hours I watched deer as they continued pouring out of the woods onto the edges of the meadow to graze. Not wanting to move for fear of spooking the deer and disturbing the woods, I sat statue-like, trying to ward off the evening cold snap. Deer were more active on this afternoon than any other during the hunt, and I could see several feeding into the middle of fields to the north and east of my stand.

I'm not one for sitting much in stands, as I'm always curious to see what animals may be active around the next corner. Just as I persuaded myself to abandon the tree and go to spot-and-stock tactics, a little seven point buck that was walking underneath me snapped his head up, turned and faced west, into the timber.

I didn't hear or see what alerted the little buck, but the fact he turned 180 degrees and remained there for 10 minutes convinced me to stay in the tree. Finally, the faint sound of a snapping branch caught my attention. The sound came from the timber, but because it was so subtle and so distant, I questioned whether there was a prayer of seeing the source of the sound prior to darkness setting in.

Five more minutes slowly crept by and finally the sound of another snapping twig wafted through the air. This time a gray back slowly prowled through thick underbrush, its head obscured by heavy cover. Each of the deer's strides was intentionally slow and precisely placed. Though I couldn't see antlers, the demeanor of the deer left no doubt it was a buck. The question was, how big? Unlike the younger bucks who came crashing through cover to feed, this one was more sagacious.

As he slipped behind a fallen tree, I slowly positioned the muzzleloader into shooting position. Enthusiasm escalated as I waited for the deer to materialize. Finally, the tip of a moist, black nose appeared, working the wind.

Three quick strides sent him in and out of view and safely behind another fallen tree, where he stopped, out of sight. What I'd seen in that brief moment he flashed in front of me, left no doubt he was a shooter. Though not the giant deer I had hoped for, his long, even rack and forked eye-guards made him what would be my biggest whitetail ever.

Slowly stepping out from behind the tree, the buck's 12-point rack appeared more massive than I'd first anticipated. At this point it was obvious the buck was not going to follow the same trails the other deer had been traveling on, rather slip through the thick poplars which offered cover. With darkness only minutes away, the time was now. With a solid rest on the frame of my stand, and given the fact the shot was barely over 50 yards, the outcome was inevitable. Heart thumping, the gun felt surprisingly steady as I applied trigger pressure.

Pushed by a cloud of white smoke, the 295 grain PowerBelt bullet hit the mark. Blood streamed from the crease behind the buck's shoulder as he went on a final sprint into the forest from which he came. Watching the prized deer crash through brush, he finally piled-up, not 20 yards from where I'd hit him.

Walking out of the woods, I was surprised with the amount of daylight still remaining in the open fields. Midway across the field, I was met by Maduck, Gruber and the camera man. "How big is he?" Gruber quizzed.

"How big is what?" I shivered? "I got so cold sitting in the stand I had to get out and move around."

"Knock it off," Gruber smiled. "We heard you shoot."

The moment Gruber drove back into camp with a replacement camera, I shot my buck.

I was more than pleased with my muzzleloader whitetail. The only regret was that we were unable to capture the final moments of action on film,

The only time in four days I didn't have a camera man with me, and I kill a whopper whitetail. Go figure.

In the dark we filmed a quick recovery of my deer. To be honest, his rack was bigger than I'd thought, dwarfed by his body that would be pushing the 300 pound mark. It was the biggest bodied deer I'd ever taken, and it made his 150-plus-inch rack appear smaller than it really was.

I left camp the next morning, when Gruber's hunt began. He took the time to get the job done right, and ended up securing a good TV show which later aired on Outdoor America. Though he didn't get a giant buck, he took a nice representative deer for the area.

The outfitter booked multiple hunts off the show, and Wolf Creek Productions made good on their promise of putting together a quality program. Still, when I watched that show, I couldn't help but recall all the big bucks that weren't shown due to a camera malfunction. Fortunately, everyone was happy in the end, and that's all that really mattered.

Chapter 20:

Hog Wild In Texas

There are many lessons to learn in life and many settings where learning takes place. Hunting excursions are one of those situations that open up the doors to learning. On this, one of our first family outings with the focus of hunting for a TV show, there was no shortage of teachable moments.

Seconds after pulling into the Texas ranch house, a truck came barreling in behind us. Skidding to a stop, dust flying, the door quickly popped open and the driver jumped out. Running around to the back of the truck, the driver grabbed something, circled around the other side of the truck, then came to greet us.

Juan, the driver, a stalky young man dressed in camouflage, a permanent smile pasted on his face, reached out his hand. "Welcome to the Callaghan Ranch," he cheered, my oldest son's right hand in his, rattle snake in his left hand. "Look, we just got dinner!" he announced, holding up the snake.

My boys looked at me and didn't know what to think. Then my wife looked at me with that, "What have you gotten us into?" glare.

"Don't worry," I encouraged, "its head has been chopped off, it's harmless. You boys can even go play with it if you'd like." My wife gave me that weird look, again, and the boys were off chasing after Juan. For more than an hour they played with that snake in the powder-dry dirt outside our bunkhouse. If you've ever had the experience of seeing a decapitated snake, you know they continue wriggling and slithering for hours, even reacting to being touched.

With the level of excitement the boys showed, and their interest in the headless reptile, I knew it was going to be a fun week. We had chicken for dinner that night, at least that's what the cook told us it was.

No matter where my job takes me, I always yearn for my family to come along to share the experiences. From the unique scenery to the history, from the animals to the people, each destination I travel to holds something very special. Due to my intense spring and fall traveling schedule, however, and some of the remote places we're in, it's not always possible for the family to come along.

This hunt was different. It was early April and all four of us, Tiffany, Braxton, Kazden and I, flew to south Texas where we'd spend the week hunting hogs and javelina. Bret Stuart, our camera man, was also on this trip with the intent of filming an episode of Western Adventures.

Bret and his family live 10 minutes from us, in Oregon, and we've shared many fond memories. Bret is one of the top salmon and steelhead fishing guides in our area, and he and I have spent a lot of time on the water over the years. In fact, both of my boys, at age four, caught their first summer steelhead while fishing with Bret and I. He's a good man with a big heart, and my boys love being around him.

There was so much I wanted the kids to get out of this trip, I had to be careful not to be too forceful. This is where having Tiffany along really helped keep a balance. Braxton was a few weeks away from his 7th birthday, Kazden only a few days from turning five. They were young, no question, but more than ready to experience what a different part of the country was like.

Not only did I want the boys to see the land, the animals and meet new people, but I wanted them to see me, their dad, at work. Though they'd both been involved with shooting TV around home, they hadn't really seen all that's involved. When it comes to traveling, depending on so many other people and the long days we put in when actually filming away from home, my job becomes just that, a job. Braxton had a good idea of what we do when filming hunts when he starred in a couple shows in Texas the previous fall. His experience helped, for sure.

Filming a hunt for television and simply going on a hunt are two different things. Not wanting to convolute things while in the field, Bret and I decided it would be best to take the boys on their hunts, one at a time. We'd start first with Braxton, since he had some experience, was a bit older and is a very good rifle shot.

Wild boar were our first target, and for this, we waited until evening when the pigs were more active. In the last couple hours of the day, the hogs come out of the dense brush and scour the road for fresh grass. It had been a wet spring, and there was plenty of green to relish in.

This hunt, like all of them on this trip, would be by way of spot and stalk. I wanted the boys to hone this skill, as it's our primary approach on big game animals throughout the West, where we do most of our filming. If we had to, we'd corn the roads, but given the vast amount of lush grass, this wasn't likely going to be necessary.

On one of the first roads we walked down, we saw a pair of black hogs. Just the sight of them got Braxton excited, which got everyone else excited. When we first saw the pigs, they were about 400 yards out, moving away from us. Going fast, we tried closing the gap, but it was tough given how flat and open it was. When the pigs put their heads down, we'd move. The going was slow at times, but proved a good lesson on patience for Braxton.

At one point we got to within about 200 yards of the hogs, then two sows and their litters fed out of the brush. Two more boars followed. Behind us, several pigs were now feeding in the road. In all, we had more than 20 black hogs feeding within sight. It was a great start.

Wanting Braxton to get a boar, we now had several other sets of eyes to contend with. Again, patience was a virtue. We also had to time our moves, for fear of spooking every pig back into the brush. After nearly and hour of stalking, and covering 700 yards, we finally got Braxton to within 100 yards of a boar. Just as he readied to shoot, another momma and her piglets came out of the brush and started grazing between us and the boar. Braxton had no shot and fully understood why.

As the sow and little ones fed down the road away from us, the boar followed. Getting ready to make another move on him, the boar stopped, turned and began feeding our direction. Braxton was already in shooting position, firm on his bipod. Now it was just a matter of time.

The closer the hog came, the more excited Braxton grew. There were several moments where he wanted to shoot, and could have, but Bret wanted to get as much footage of the hog before giving the okay to pull the trigger. This is one element where filming a hunt for TV and hunting without a camera are quite different. Had it not been for TV, Braxton could have shot the pig five minutes earlier. But in order to make good TV, we need as much live footage of the animal as possible, and that takes time. There are also risks, for if the animal busts you, there are no retakes. Reading animal behavior is crucial at this point, not only for making quality TV, but for getting the job done, properly.

Fortunately, the boar kept moving our direction. Once he got to 80 yards, Bret gave us the green light to shoot. The pig kept his head down, continuing to feed our way. The moment the pig turned his head to the left, Braxton put the tip of his Trijicon AccuPoint on the money and fired. The lightening fast bullet from his .204 hit perfectly, dropping the hog on the spot. The boar, about 150 pounds, was solid black with a nice little set of tusks.

138

Braxton helped gut the pig, just as I expect him to do with any animal he shoots. Leaving the hog along the side of the road, we headed back to get the rig. About halfway there, another group of pigs worked into the road in front of us. We were losing light, fast. In fact, it was too dark to film.

"Go ahead and take one anyway," Jeff Fischer, the ranch manager, told Braxton. "But it's too dark to film it," Braxton pointed out. "Don't worry about it, we have lots of hogs you can hunt, just go get him before it's too dark to shoot," Jeff insisted.

Braxton looked at me with a questioning smile. He knew Dad never gets to shoot animals unless they're on film, and was excited at the thought of being able to get this bonus hog. A short stalk around some brush and cactus found us in position, 75 yards from the pod of pigs. When an adult hog stepped out into the open, Braxton made another perfect shot, instantly folding the pig. It was such low light, the hogs were tough to see with the na-

At age six, Braxton spot and stalked his way to these two Texas hogs.
He made perfect, one-shot kills on both of them.

ked eye. Had it not been for the illuminated reticle in his Trijicon, Braxton would not have been able to make that shot. Talk about adding confidence to a child's hunting experience.

Driving into camp that night, Tiffany and Kazden came to greet us. Braxton was elated, and all smiles over his success. I couldn't have been more proud. After snapping some photos, we skinned the hogs and got them hanging in the cooler. At the time, Tiffany was writing a big game cookbook and we needed all the wild pig meat we could get. The lean, flavorful meat is a great addition to the other game we eat.

The next morning we'd head out after Javelina. We got Kazden on several stalks, but no shot opportunities presented themselves. One of the problems was how much javelina move around when feeding. They're a high-strung animal, and seem to never hold still.

Kazden was shooting a .17 HMR, and we wanted him to take a head shot in order to ensure a clean kill. The hard part was getting the javelina to hold their heads still. Finally, after five blown stalks, we got to within 40 yards of a group of feeding javelina. Kazden felt good, securely set in his bipod. Just as he pulled the trigger, the javelina swung from right to left and the bullet sailed right by his head. A clean miss.

It was a long morning for Kazden and I could sense he was growing frustrated with getting so close so many times, yet not being able to get a shot at a still target. It was time for a break.

While Bret went off filming other hunters in camp, Tiffany and I took the boys to see what a working ranch is like. The habitat in South Texas is unlike anything the boys had ever seen. Virtually every plant has thorns. They were intrigued with the variety of cacti, and spent hours whittling away at them with their pocket knives. In fact, every day we had to have cactus carving time. Now, years later, the boys still talk about cutting up cacti in Texas.

Because the hogs and javelina are pretty crepuscular in their behavior – active during the first and last minutes of daylight – we were able to have plenty of time to explore the area during mid-day. In this flat country, less than 30 miles from the Mexico border, there were no mountains, even hills as we knew them back home. The boys thought that was interesting, how flat the area was; how different this place was from home.

Jeff even took the boys to his favorite arrowhead grounds, and let them have free-reign. After filtering through I don't know how many pounds of little rocks, finally, Braxton found a single arrowhead. He carried it in his pocket the rest of the trip, never letting it out of his possession. It still sits on a shelf in his bedroom.

One day after lunch, we went to another side of the ranch, not something you do quickly when the property encompasses nearly 100,000 acres. There we saw a stockyard full of domestic pigs. Braxton and Kazden spent nearly two hours feeding, watching and enjoying these pigs and their antics. They especially loved the little piglets and got a kick out of watching the 600 pound boars wallow around. We also played with baby goats and rabbits every day.

Every evening, dinner was prepared on an open grill, over a hot bed of mesquite coals. Virtually all the meat we eat is wild game we gather ourselves, and we do a lot of grilling at home. The boys enjoy the taste of grilled meat and were keen to pick up on the different flavor the mesquite offered. They couldn't get enough of it at the end of every long day.

They also enjoyed sitting around the fire, listening to adults share their stories. The overall experiences the boys were having was everything I'd hoped it would be. For them to get away from home and learn how other people live their lives, what other parts of our great country are like, and how Dad goes about his daily work routine, were all invaluable impressions made on the boys that week.

Kazden was wanting to get a javelina before turning five, which gave us one day, for the following day we'd be celebrating his birthday on this ranch. Not wanting him to face any further frustrations with having to try and head-shoot the fidgeting javelina, I made a decision to switch out barrels on his Thompson Center G2. Replacing the .17 HMR barrel with the .204, now he'd be able to shoot for the body. This made all the difference.

Though Kazden had never fired the .204, the scope setup was the same as on the .17 barrel, so he knew what things looked like. The bipod was also the same. The only change was the caliber. While the .204 is a much louder gun and packs a bit of a wallop, he'd seen his brother shoot it enough to know what to expect. I figured the adrenaline rush of focusing on the shot would ease the surprise of the recoil.

The first drove of javelina we put the move on gave us the slip, melting into the thorn bush before we could get within range. Then we got on a pair of adults, both males, both worth shooting. Moving quickly down the side of an open road, we hurried to get within range of the drifting animals. Just as I was about to give up hope, the pair stopped, turned and started coming our direction.

At just over 100 yards, Kazden clearly picked up both javelina in his scope. He wanted to shoot then, but I wanted them to come closer. Once

My youngest son, Kazden, prepares for a shot at a javelina. At age four, Kazden became the youngest hunter to ever take a javelina on this Texas ranch. He dropped the animal on the spot with one shot from his .204.

they hit 75 yards, it was time to get ready for the shot. Kazden was set with one knee on the ground, gun rock-solid on the bipod. I took one final reading with the rangefinder: 70 yards.

"Shoot him right on the collar?" Kazden confirmed before pulling the trigger on the biggest male that was now broadside to us. I was impressed with his taking the time to recall what we'd studied during our range-time back home. "That's right," I whispered, "take him whenever you're... "Boom!" Kazden shot before I could even finish getting my words out.

The shot was perfect and it put the javelina down on the spot. "I got one, I got one!" Kazden kept shouting the moment the javelina dropped. Laughing, smiling and swapping hugs and high-fives, he said nothing about the gun's recoil.

Kazden couldn't get up to that javelina fast enough. He was enamored with the size of the animal's tusks, coarse hair and small hooves that looked like deer feet. He was also intrigued with the little gland on the lower back of the javelina and what it was used for. We spent several minutes learning about the anatomy of these unique animals, and Kazden was soaking it all in like a sponge. Teachable moments like this wouldn't happen were it not for hunting.

During Kazden's stalk, Tiffany and Braxton stayed safely behind, enjoying the action from a distance. Being able to have the whole family around Kazden's first game animal meant the world to him, as it did to all of us.

Making our way back to the bunkhouse, an unexpected opportunity presented itself. Ahead, a half-dozen javelina were feeding in the road. Quickly, Braxton and I made a short stalk and got to within range. Then the javelina went into the brush. Eventually they popped out, nearly 150 yards away. Braxton felt he could make the shot, and he did, putting the pig down with one well-placed bullet.

The pictures of those two boys, together, with their javelina, are among my favorite photos we've ever captured. Their smiles say it all, and the fact they executed perfect stalks followed by precise, one-shot kills, and all with the TV camera looming over their heads, made the entire adventure something we will all remember, forever.

The Haugen boys shared many fond memories with camera man, Bret Stuart, over the years. We were all happy with the way this TV show came together.

As for Tiffany, I really wanted her to shoot her first javelina. It didn't happen, but it wasn't for a lack of effort. Tiffany was set on getting her javelina with a bow, or nothing. Over the course of the week she had several good stalks, but unfortunately a shot opportunity never presented itself. She likely could have taken one while sitting over bait, but chose to stick to the spot and stalk approach. If nothing else, Tiffany's not filling a tag gave the boys an added boost of confidence by knowing they got their javelina and mom didn't. It was a friendly family competition which can be healthy in the right situation. In this case, it definitely encouraged the boys to take their efforts seriously. To see what her two sons had just accomplished made Tiffany more proud than if she'd have pulled the trigger, herself, and that's what this trip was all about.

Heading back to the San Antonio airport, we all had a great time reliving the experiences we'd just had. But before hopping on the plane we took a few hours to tour the Alamo. Both Braxton and Kazden are intrigued with the famed lives led by frontiersmen like Davy Crockett and James Bowie. For them, the learning opportunities just kept coming, and they enjoyed every second of it.

Every time I look at the bleached skulls of the boys' javelinas adorning our trophy room, I see more than just bones. I see a week of priceless memories that left lasting impressions on my sons' lives, impressions that would not have been ingrained were it not for hunting.

Chapter 21:

Big Bruins Of Quinault

For hunters, there's nothing like discovering new land. On this black bear quest, I became one of the first non-native people to hunt reservation land in more than 150 years. What I experienced surpassed my wildest expectations.

A slight breeze whirled through the massive fir trees in which I sat, inundating the air with a fresh smell of sea salt. The tips of sword ferns delicately danced in the shadows, confirming the wind was still in my favor. An unseasonably dry forest floor then crackled, signifying a bear was moving toward me.

It was my third calling setup – the previous two locations proved fruitless. As the bear circled in the brush, it was obvious he was trying to wind me. Toning down the calls from intense wails to mild cries and squeaks, the bear finally couldn't resist and poked his head from the brush.

Ears erect, nostrils pumping, the bruin searched for the source of the sounds. He knew something was not right, and though I had a shot at the bear's throat, it was not one I wanted to take.

"I'm on him," whispered Dave Arabia, my camera man. Dave and I have shared many great hunts around the world, and have come to know one another well. On this journey, we were filming an episode for Adventures Abroad, a TV series I hosted during it's first year on the Outdoor Channel. The frustrating part, Dave could see much more of the bear than I could. Dave was to the left of me about 10-feet, and I simply didn't have the same view he did. Just one more step from the brush was all I needed that bear to take.

As he lifted his right front paw to take a step, he pivoted on his hind quarters, turned 180° and melted back into the forest. No shot was fired, and in retrospect I'm kicking myself, for he was a bear that was pushing 400 pounds with a blocky-head I still dream about.

The next evening found Dave and I in the same area, trying to call in a bear. I'd hoped to see the big boar again, but despite my calling efforts, nothing came tearing out of the brush. Then, at last light a small bear wandered out of the trees and started heading our direction.

Intense, high-pitched squeals kept his attention. He wasn't a big bear, but I didn't care, for calling in any bear with a predator call is a rush. Once he committed to making his way into the opening, I knew I'd better be ready to take a shot.

This is where Trijicon's scopes are worth their weight in gold, for in the extreme low light conditions I faced, not to mention a black colored bear against a black forest background, the illuminated apex of the scope's reticle was easy to see and tuck tight behind the bear's shoulder. When the bear turned and offered me a broadside shot, the .375 JDJ did the rest. I was halfway to my two bear limit on this hunt.

Dan Leuthold with one of many big bears we've taken off
Quinault tribal lands over the years.

It was early spring, and I was hunting on the Quinault Indian Reservation, a place that had not been hunted by non-tribal members since 1855. Actually, this was my second spring of hunting in this grand land. The year prior was the first year it opened to outside hunting and on that six day hunt I saw 23 bears, nearly all boars. Of those, at least one-third would likely have made Pope & Young, with three probably qualifying for the Boone & Crockett book.

Nestled on the coast of Washington's Olympic Peninsula, the 200,000-plus acres of tribal land encompasses some 350 square miles. But what's great about the Quinault – besides its monster bears – is that hunting pressure had been extremely light over the years, bear densities were high and baiting is allowed. In fact, this is the only place in Washington state where bait could be used for bears.

Due to the lack of hunting pressure by tribal members over the years, bears are exceeding the carrying capacity of the land. Competition for food is tight and many bears have resorted to munching on the cambium layer of Douglas fir and cedar trees to sustain themselves.

Logging is big business on the reservation, and with intensive studies revealing that bears were annually causing a conservative estimation of one million dollars in annual timber loss, the decision was made to open the land to non-tribal hunters. It's a prime example of how hunting can be used as a tool of game and forest management.

From what I'd seen on my first hunt, and now half way through my second hunt on the Quinault, I was quickly concluding it could well be one of the country's best kept bear secrets. There was no question this place was going to give some competition to Prince of Wales and Vancouver islands.

With one tag filled and another burning a hole in my pocket, the next evening found me 15-feet above ground, sitting in a tree stand. It was a new bait site, one that had been set by guide, Jaime Lorton, a couple day's prior to my arrival. The first night I sat, nothing showed up, but previous sign revealed at least one bear was in the area.

The following night I was back in the same tree, smelling the salty air and hearing the crashing of Pacific Ocean waves hitting the rocky cliffs less than 100 yards from my stand. The first two bears that came in were small, but their demeanor told me a bigger, more dominant bear was likely in the area. The next bear to come in was a brute, and I didn't hesitate shooting.

At the shot, the bear went only a short distance before being swallowed by a very dense forest. While waiting for things to settle before hopping on the blood trail, two more bears came in.

*Far from the biggest bear I've taken on the Quinault Reservation,
this one fell to a muzzleloader. My two biggest bears have come with a bow,
and others with a rifle.*

Darkness was falling and with four bears now surrounding the bait, I knew I had to make a move. If not found quickly, bear meat spoils fast, and bear is one of our families favorite meats.

Making plenty of noise as Dave and I descended from the tree, the bears on the bait ran only a short distance. With the rapid loss of daylight, every shadow in front of us materialized into a potential bear. When we broke out our flashlights, even more eerie shadows were cast.

We could hear bears snapping branches and popping their teeth over the crashing waves in the background. We were unsure whether they wanted us, the bear I'd just shot, or the bait we'd been hunting over. Fortunately, we quickly found our bear and dragged his carcass to a little opening where I could skin and quarter him.

With Dave standing lookout with a flashlight, I've never field dressed and boned out a bear so quickly in my life. It was well after dark before I finished the work, stuffed the meat in my pack, threw the hide over my shoulder and took off. Dave had all his camera gear gathered, and we wasted no time hitting the trail. Talking as we went, we quickly covered ground. The presence of multiple bears does that to a guy...that's what makes bear hunting so fun.

During the four days spent in camp that spring, 11 of 12 hunters fired shots at bears. Four bears over the 300 pound mark were taken, one over 400 pounds. One of those bears weighed 375 pounds and was taken by Monte Kenning. Monte had read about the Quinault in a magazine article I had written, and drove to the hunt from his Nebraska home. The most inspiring part of meeting Monte, he was a paraplegic. Paralyzed from the waist down, he took his giant bear while seated in a blind, in his wheelchair.

While the Quinault is a high percentage hunt, it's not a slam-dunk on trophy class bears every time you set foot in the woods. It's hunting, and anything can happen, just like anywhere else bears roam.

On my first hunt to the Quinault, I had one mammoth boar stride within four yards of me. Huddled behind a few twigs that made up a rudimentary ground blind, I held my bow, but could not get a shot due to a poor camera angle – we were filming a TV show then, too. The 500-plus pound giant busted me and took off. When it was all over, I don't know who was shaking more.

I did manage two good bears the first time I hunted the Quinault, one with my bow, one with a muzzleloader. Both of those bears were taken while hunting with veteran guide, Carl Lorton. I've hunted with Carl several times, and continue planning hunts with him, even as I write these words.

For me, the Quinault is a magical place with deep meaning. I love hunting with the Native American guides and getting the opportunity to know their families and learn their culture. This part of the experience takes me back to the years I lived and hunted with the Inupiat Eskimos in the Alaskan arctic.

Then there's the scenery. The rainforest reminds me of other such habitats I've spent time in, both where I lived in Indonesia, and where I've traveled in South America. The lush, green ferns and massive fir trees also take me back to where I grew up hunting, on the western slopes of Oregon's Cascades Range.

Monty Kenning, a paraplegic, took this massive spring bear from a ground blind. It's beasts like this that attract bear hunters from around the country to this land on Washington's Olympic Peninsula.

Simply put, the Quinault is one of those places I never tire of experiencing. There's a reason I keep going back to this mystic land, and why I'm now introducing my wife and sons to what this special place has to offer.

Chapter 22:

White Bird Whitetail

I love hunting anything out West, including whitetails.
In Idaho, where the land is immense, rugged and unforgiving,
it's whitetail hunting unlike anywhere else in the country.
Include a land that's rich in Native American history, and the
experience becomes even more profound.

I'd been sitting in the tree stand for three hours, and with only a few min-utes of light remaining, finally saw a whitetail buck. He was chasing a doe, and as he ran through the thick brush, it was hard telling how big he was.

His husky, gray body obviously revealed he was a mature buck, but I struggled to see his rack. Then he broke into the open. From my side-view, his dark, heavy rack extended past his nose and his tines were tall. Through the scope I could see he was a perfect 5x5 with eye guards, what my eastern buddies would call a 12-point.

Readying for a shot the moment the buck stopped, the words I didn't want to hear, inevitably came. "We're out of light," whispered Bret Stuart, my camera man of three years. Then the buck stopped and gave me a perfect look, but I couldn't shoot.

When filming hunting shows, keep in mind, the high-end cameras we rely on are not intended for outside use. They're also not designed to gather light, like some of the optics we use. This means many of the camera models actually lose light faster than the human eye. The result, we lose the best 15 minutes of each morning and evening hunt, all for the sake of getting the kill shot on film.

I've become somewhat used to the fact we have to sacrifice our best moments of hunting for the sake of making good TV, but on this buck, I struggled. Staring at him through the scope, I did some quick calculating.

Twice I ran the numbers, and twice I came up with a rack that would have scored over 170-inches. He was a whopper of a buck, and I had to let him walk. No kill shot on film, no TV show, that's our rule.

The good thing, it was the first of a seven day hunt and I felt confident we'd see the buck again. In fact, given how rutty he acted, I was almost certain we'd see him again. We did, twice.

The very next morning he ran right by our stand, hot on the tail of a doe, but again it was too low of light to film. Three days later, he appeared about 9:00 a.m., over 400 yards away, too far to chance a shot from a tree stand. That was the last we saw of him.

During those five days of hunting, we did see nearly a dozen other bucks I would have shot had it not been for the big daddy hanging around. I'd been bitten by the whitetail bug, and wanted this monster buck in the worst way.

Then business obligations took over. With two days remaining in the hunt, I had two whitetail tags in my pocket. I was sent there to get two TV shows for our Western Adventures program. We had plenty of support footage, but no kills. It was time to abandon the big buck, and I knew it.

Moving to another valley, we spotted a dandy 10-point buck – oops, I mean 4x4 with eye guards. He was bedded atop a shale slide, beneath an alder thicket. At just over 400 yards, he was a long way for a shot, but it was impossible to get any closer.

Then the deer spooked and started running up the opposite hillside. It was open terrain, and as Bret got situated on his tripod, I did the same in my shooting sticks. "I'm on the doubler," confirmed Bret. "Take him whenever you want, I'm on him the whole way," he encouraged.

Hitting the doubler told me Bret had the camera on the highest power, meaning viewers would be able to see the buck even though it was so far off. Ranging a big rock near where the buck was heading, I got a reading of 460 yards. Knowing time was of the essence, I decided to take the shot.

The buck was facing straight away, and the fact the hillside he climbed was so steep, the entire length of his body was exposed to me. Knowing I had such a generous kill zone to work with, I knew it was now or never.

The deer was trotting, but not overly fast due to the steepness of the mountain he chose to climb. Cranking the scope to high power, putting the tip of the Trijicon AccuPoint 2.5-10x56 on the end of the buck's nose, I touched one off. The .300 Winchester Magnum echoed heavily across the rocky canyon, filling the silence with resounding authority.

The instant the bullet slammed into the base of the deer's neck, he tipped over backwards, and rolled. Because it was such steep country, the buck continued rolling and rolling. He tumbled over 100 yards, coming to rest in a patch of wild rose hips.

At 463 yards, it wasn't the most ideal shot to take, either for myself or for TV, but it worked. Approaching the buck, we were amazed to find all his tines intact.

By the time we got the buck off the rugged mountain, we had only that afternoon and another full day to hunt before the whitetail season came to a close. That afternoon I couldn't help but return to where we last saw the big buck. He didn't show up.

The next morning, a heavy-racked 3x3 with nice eye guards gave us a shot opportunity. He was chasing a doe through some tall masses of rose hips,

Taken on the move at 463 yards across a gaping canyon, this was one of the most impressionable moments we ever captured on film. Note the high, rugged country these Idaho whitetails live in.

*On the final day of the season I ended up with this beautiful Idaho whitetail.
Though he wasn't the big buck we'd held out for, we were more than pleased to
have filled a tag.*

and when he paused in an opening, I had to take him. At 306 yards, the rifle
again connected and our second show was complete.

Tim Craig, owner of Boulder Creek Outfitters was pleased, though
a bit nervous that we drug out the hunts so long. The good part, he
invited us back the following year to try and find that big whitetail
buck.

In late November, 2007 I was back with Boulder Creek Outfitters filming the hunt for Outdoor America, and we were looking for that monster
whitetail just west of Orofino. On the first morning, I watched a 140-inch
brute of a buck, but held off in hopes of finding our big buck. We hunted the
area hard for five days but never saw him.

Tim suggested we spend the final days of the hunt on some private land
he had leased near the historic little town of White Bird, Idaho, a few hours
south of where we'd been hunting. It was hard giving up hopes on the big
buck, but no one had seen him all season and the chances seemed slim of
finding him.

This setup is what I took all three of my Idaho whitetails with over the course of two seasons.

I'd heard a great deal about the White Bird property and the big whitetails living in this area, so was enthusiastic to see it. On the first day, all day, we watched whitetails, mule deer and elk. The place was packed with animals, and many of the whitetails were rutting. We saw some good bucks, but nothing worth pulling the trigger on.

Then, on the final morning of the hunt, the rut kicked into overdrive. The first thirteen deer we saw were bucks, including a whopper that carried impressive eye guards. Matt Craig, my ace guide on this hunt, didn't even need to look at the buck through the spotting scope to confirm he was a shooter. Neither did I.

While Matt kept a watchful eye on the buck, my camera man for this fall season, Sam Potter, and I snuck into a dry creekbed and moved quickly to close the distance. Popping up over a slight embankment, we were relieved to find the buck hadn't moved. In fact, he was fighting with another buck and had no clue we were there.

Breaking free from locked antlers, the lesser buck sprinted away from us, the big buck right on his tail. When the big buck slowed, then stopped, I was already in the sticks, ready to shoot. At just over 170 yards, the bullet took out the buck's heart. He ran only a short distance before expiring.

My best western whitetail to date, this one was taken in White Bird, Idaho. In the background is the famous battle field where the war against the Nez Perce was launched, 130 years prior.

The near perfect, 5x5 rack was even bigger than I'd thought. His exceptional mass and impressive tine length taped out to about 150-inches of antler. No, he wasn't the 170-inch buck we'd hoped for, but he was the next best thing and I couldn't have been more elated.

What really gave this buck special meaning to me was not only his size, but where he was taken. From where we snapped photos of the gorgeous deer, we could look across the valley of White Bird and see the very spot where this place made history. It was here on June 17, 1877, that the famous battle of White Bird took place, launching what became one of the country's most recognized wars against Native Americans, Chief Joseph and the Nez Perce.

Standing there, imagining what this valley looked like 130 years prior, was an awe-inspiring feeling. For me, having the honor to hunt it and take such a magnificent whitetail buck, made the moment that much more heartfelt. Once again, hunting took me to a powerful place I otherwise would not have seen, and provided me with an experience I'll never forget.

Chapter 23:

The Porcupine Buck

A year following my first whitetail deer hunt with
Shane Weiler in eastern Montana, I was back.
This time, our target was mule deer.

Shadows cast by towering rock cliffs and leafless trees grew tall on the valley floor as the sun swiftly dropped on the horizon. From where we sat, 12 bucks could be seen – two were shooters. It was mid-November, 2003, the height of the mule deer rut, and Shane and I sat glassing the broken hills between Forsyth and Miles City.

As the does emerged from the hill country, worked their way through sagebrush then descended upon the creek bottoms to feed, the bucks soon followed. This is where we sat, waiting for deer to move our way.

A good four point first caught Shane's sharp eyes. "He's nice, but we can do better," he whispered without lifting his eye from the spotting scope.

Seconds later, "There's another good buck, and there are two more fighting over there," Shane pointed out. Then, silhouetted atop a rim of weathered granite, the dark configuration of a perfect bowl-shaped set of antlers caught my eye.

"That's the one I want," I informed Shane. "We can do better, he's only about 25-inches wide," he replied. Closer inspection revealed the buck had pretty good mass, and though his forks weren't deep, he was, no doubt, a good buck. The classic configuration of his rack screamed mule deer.

Right then and there I told myself, "If this buck comes to within range, I'm taking him." If something bigger came along, great, but I wasn't planning on holding out.

It was more the setting, and the feel of the moment, which made me want this buck. In less than an hour, we'd seen over a dozen bucks in this one spot, but there was just something about this big boy that tugged at my heart. His

white muzzle, thick torso and overall demeanor exuded the confidence of a king. He gave off an air of being a dominant buck all others bowed down to. Record book qualifier or not, the more I watched this buck, the more I wanted him.

It took him nearly an hour to reach the sage-lined field, where the other bucks were now chasing dozens of does. Then the majestic buck lifted his head, lip-curled and made a beeline into the corner of the field. He'd caught wind of a doe in heat, and when he made his move, all the other bucks stepped aside. He was still well over 1,000 yards away, but at least he was getting closer.

We were losing daylight, fast, and since we were filming the hunt for a TV show, time

I've shared many fun adventures with good friend, Shane Weiler. I love hunting with this man. Shane took this buck to put some meat in his freezer.

was becoming precious. "If you want that buck, we're going to have to run up this creek bed, through that patch of trees and skirt the ditch line near the field," Shane made clear. "Even then we might get busted, but we have to move now if you want to try and make it happen!"

I wanted this buck, bad, but in a way, I didn't want the hunt to end, either. During the previous few days we'd looked over more muley bucks than I'd ever seen on a single hunt. I was still second-guessing myself for passing up a buck that was all of 30-inches wide. Though he was wide, he was only a 3x4, and I opted to pass. That was a hard one, as he was in a stalkable position and would have made for great footage.

One thing that's important to understand, when we're out filming hunts for television shows, the size of the animal is just one element taken into consideration before pulling the trigger. There are so many other factors to toil with.

Is the animal relaxed? Is he in a position that will make for a good, quality sequence? Is the lighting right or will the sun shift and botch our view by the time we can reach the animal? What if a monster animal presents a

shot in the first moments of the hunt and we have no supporting footage to help build a solid show? How many more days do we have to hunt, and are we seeing enough good animals that we can realistically wait? These are only some of the questions that run through our minds on every single hunt.

Perhaps the question that looms heaviest when filming a show is, "What if we pass an opportunity then don't get another chance?" Shooting TV shows isn't cheap, and it's far from easy. Don't get me wrong, at this point in my life I can't imagine doing anything else for a living, nor do I want to. The pressures of TV are intense, and force me to think about hunting from a whole different perspective than simply going out for the purpose of putting meat in the freezer.

This is where my desire and willingness to work hard to get a job done, pays off. I like having camera men with the same characteristics, and that's not always easy to find. Staying focused and being driven to complete a job is essential, no matter what your occupation. Sometimes the demands are great in the TV hunting business, and because we're pursuing animals that are out of our control, unforeseen stress often escalates.

There are families to consider, not only in the frame of time I could be spending with my wife and kids, but the same for the camera man as well as the guide and/or outfitter who may be with us. The producers and the entire production crew are also on our minds, for they are up against deadlines, and the last thing we want is for them to have to pull-off many nights of consecutive editing to put together a show.

These are just some of the things that race through my mind when shooting TV shows. I try not to think about the potential value of a show to an outfitter, for this can range into the hundreds of thousands of dollars on high end hunts; revenue they make off booking hunts from the show. There's a fine line of separation between taking an animal to fill a tag and taking an animal to complete a TV show. I like taking big animals, and try to do that on every hunt; that's a personal thing. However, combining hunting with business means things don't always work out the way I'd like them to. Often, the big bucks get away.

On this hunt, things were coming together nicely, and I tried maintaining focus on this particular buck. The more I watched him, the more I wanted him. I knew there were bigger bucks around, but who knows if we'd ever see them. If we were going to try and close the deal on this buck, we had to move fast.

A quarter-mile sprint got us within 700 yards of the buck, still not even close. By now, deer surrounded us, including six bucks in the 20 to 24-inch range. As we continued running toward the target buck, I realized the only way we'd get a chance at him would be if he turned and started prancing our

way. Fortunately, the doe our buck was following turned our direction and the buck pushed her, hard. My wish was coming true.

I see it as fate, as my view on life is that everything happens for a reason. That doe could have gone countless directions, but she moved toward us instead. I took that as a sign that this buck was meant for me.

At 339 yards from where we lay in the ditch, the doe stopped, squatted and urinated. The buck lurched his head down, smelled, lip-curled and rub-urinated. This gave me time to hit him once again with the rangefinder. Exactly 339 yards.

Things were happening fast, as we had less than a minute of filming light remaining. While the camera man, Bret Stuart, hustled into position, I slid the .300 Remington Ultra Mag' into a firm rest on the frozen ground, then

Don Taylor created the perfect end to our mule deer hunt by dropping this nice buck with one shot amidst another stunning Montana sunset.

A year after taking a nice whitetail, I was back in eastern Montana and tagged this handsome mule deer.

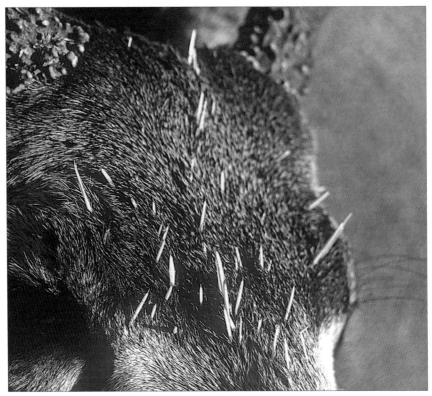

A closer look at the deer's face shows why we dubbed him the porcupine buck.

lay prone. Bodies warm from the run we'd just made, the minus 8° temperatures didn't phase me as I settled in for the shot.

As soon as Bret gave me the green light, I pulled the trigger. The buck folded in his tracks.

The animal was beautiful, his dark antlers and impressive eye-guards setting him apart from other bucks in the drainage. Closer inspection revealed an even bigger surprise, as he'd been in a recent battle with a porcupine.

Fresh quills protruding from his forehead, some very near his eye, only added to the already fond experience of this adventure. He wasn't the biggest buck in the area, but he was one of the most memorable mule deer I've taken on one of the most enjoyable deer hunts of my life.

Following my hunt, I accompanied Don Taylor, one of Shane's longtime friends, into the hill country north of Forsyth. Don hunts this section of Montana every year. He's hunted around the world, but has a deep passion for his open-country mule deer hunting. Following a long stalk on a nice 4x5 buck, Don made a perfect, one-shot kill. It was the perfect ending to a great hunt.

Chapter 24

$12 Million Blacktail

*When I shot my first Columbia blacktail deer, at age 12,
my dad was by my side. I will never forget that special moment.
On this hunt, almost 30 years to the day later, I was by his side
and he was holding the tag on this memorable hunt.*

I grew up hunting Columbia blacktails in Oregon's McKenzie River Valley, on the southeast edge of the famed Willamette Valley. This region is rich in blacktail history and today it continues kicking-out big bucks, just as it has for centuries.

My family has been hunting this terrain since the 1950s. My wife, Tiffany's side of the family, actually homesteaded in this valley in the 1800s. Our blacktail roots run deep.

Blacktail habitat along this region of the western Cascade foothills is dense and rugged, making for what I believe to be among the toughest habitat to hunt in North America. It's not unusual for hunters to go days, even an entire season, without seeing a mature blacktail buck. The blacktail's secretive ways, and the fact they live in such thick terrain makes them among the most challenging big game I've hunted anywhere in the world.

When I started filming Columbia blacktail deer hunts for television, it about drove me crazy. As if it wasn't hard enough to successfully hunt these deer on my own, now I had to do it with a camera man – sometimes two – tramping through the woods with me.

After six frustrating years, it was time to explore other options. During the fall, in order to keep on top of my filming schedule, we need to turn a TV show about every five to seven days. These hunts were taking me an average of nearly three weeks, and still, we weren't getting quality footage.

My options were simple. Either quit trying to film blacktail hunts, or go to a different blacktail habitat, one where we could see deer in open terrain. Knowing that the first choice wasn't an option, it was time to start doing some research.

I'm pretty confident when I say I've filmed more Columbia blacktail hunts for TV than any host, and that's due to the fact I want people to realize what a tough challenge these animals are to hunt. It's my belief they are the toughest big game trophy in all of North American to consistently attain, and the accolades of Jim Shockey, Craig Boddington and Bob Robb, all of whom wrote testimonials on the back cover of my book, *Trophy Blacktails: The Science of The Hunt*, seem to echo these sentiments to a certain degree.

Knowing southern Oregon to be what's likely the best place in the world to hunt trophy blacktails, and given the fact this area is less than a three hour drive from my home, I began looking there for future hunting options where we could catch the action on film. Once I met Garrett Zoller, my blacktail life changed.

Garrett was dealing in real estate, namely hunting properties, when I met him. He invited us to come down and film a blacktail hunt near his home, out of Medford, Oregon. Garrett threw out the option of helping us with a public land hunt, but when he presented us with a private land alternative, I was all ears.

Private land blacktail hunting was something neither Dad nor I had much experience with. Nearly all of our previous 73 years of combined blacktail hunting had been spent muscling through thick, wet forests on public land. When Garrett offered us the privilege to hunt on one of the most prized pieces of private land known to the blacktail hunting world, we couldn't refuse.

The property we looked to hunt was named the Dauenhauer Ranch, and is a place I've dreamed of hunting my entire life. Never in my wildest dreams did I think I'd ever hunt this place, as the Dauenhauer family has closely guarded it and wisely managed the hunting on it for generations. That's one reason the bucks grow so big there.

Technically, I wasn't hunting this land, for I held an archery tag, one to be put to use a month later, during Oregon's late archery-only blacktail season. But it was almost as if I were hunting, for Dad had the general season, over-the-counter rifle tag on this trip, and I was with him. I, along with Garrett, would play guide. We also had a camera man along.

The goal of this trip was to capture a good hunt on film in order to help Garrett and the Dauenhauer family sell this piece of real estate to an aspiring hunter or group of hunters. The asking price at the time of the hunt was 12 million dollars.

The way we shoot our programs, we knew we had to get a buck in order to produce a TV show. No kill, no TV show. It's simple. This is where the pressures of TV as business comes in. Dad knew that when the time came, he'd need to make good on the shot in order to get a TV show. The potential price tag on this project made it a far from ordinary blacktail hunt.

On the first morning of our late October hunt, we spotted a big buck bedded in tall willows in the bottom of a creek bed. By the time we reached the buck, he re-bedded, but we didn't know it until we spooked him. By then it was too late. He sprinted into some dense, low-growing oak trees and we dared not follow. Instead, we backed out of there and gave him time.

That evening we saw plenty of good bucks in another area, but not quite the caliber of the first deer we'd seen. The next morning found us glassing in the same spot where we botched the attempt on the big buck. Nothing. That evening we saw the biggest blacktail of our lives, again, in another drainage. He would have easily scored over 170-inches, but we couldn't get to him before daylight faded.

The next morning found Dad, myself and the camera man in the same spot, looking for that first buck. Again, nothing. Garrett was looking over the place where we'd seen the big buck the evening prior. He didn't find what he was looking for, either. As darkness fell, again, we separated, but didn't see either of the big bucks. The following morning found us facing the same prognosis. Blacktails will do that to you. More times than not, you'll see bucks of this caliber one time, and one time only.

But we were in southern Oregon, a land where spotting scopes could actually be used to search for deer. This open, dry habitat made for great filming, and Dad and I had seen more deer thus far in our three day hunt than we'd seen in the previous several years, combined, of hunting blacktails back home. It was like being in a Disneyland made for hunters!

On day four, all of us were back together, and right off the bat Garrett spotted that first buck. The deer was bedded less than 100 yards from where we saw him on the first day. He was laying tight to a poison oak patch, and all we could see was his rack.

This time, however, we were in a good position to stalk in from above. The buck was over a mile away, and our greatest fear was that he'd move off

Dad takes a close look at where his hunt started and ended, in the buck's bed. It was here where we spotted the deer from over a mile away, and here where we jumped him at 60 yards. The poison oak was much taller than what we initially thought, which is why the buck held here.

before we could reach him. Actually, our greatest concern was getting busted on our way to him.

There was a stretch of open land – a grassy knob about 300 yards wide – that we'd have to cross to reach the opposite gully which would then allow us to stalk this buck from behind, and above. In crossing this section of openness, we'd be vulnerable to the deer the entire time. Then we got a gift from above.

Dad tapped me on the shoulder and pointed to the rocky cliffs above us. Rolling over the mountain tops came the thickest blanket of fog imaginable. The good part, it was headed right for us.

It didn't take 10 minutes and we were engulfed in fog. Now we could safely cross through the opening without being seen. The good part, once we dropped a couple hundred feet in elevation, we were below the fog line. We thanked God for that assistance.

We were into the stalk well over an hour when we found ourselves within 60 yards of the buck. But we failed to see him though the curtain of dense poison oak.

Backing out, we had to come in from another angle in order for Dad to get a shot. Even at that, the terrain was steeper than we'd anticipated and the poison oak taller. Then the buck busted us.

The deer was on an all-out sprint downhill, and the cover was too thick to get a shot through. In the direction he was heading, he'd have to cross about a 30-yard clearing before disappearing into a jungle of tangled oak trees. We knew this opening was where Dad would have to make the shot.

The camera man was insistent that he couldn't see the buck, and urged us to hold off on the shot. Honestly, I was glad, because we were going to try for this buck, regardless of what the camera man could or could not see. You must know, in television, we have some rules to play by, one of which is that we cannot shoot at an animal on the run. I don't agree with it, but it's the rules. On this buck, I wasn't willing to play by them. I knew what was at stake here, the caliber of buck we were dealing with and how good of a shot Dad was.

Knowing the deer would not slow, I told the camera man to keep rolling tape. I also urged Dad to get on the buck and pull the trigger the moment I said. Right where the buck started into the

Walking up on his prized Columbia blacktail, the buck was even bigger than Dad imagined. It's moments like this where the hunting experience just keeps getting better.

opening, there was a slight dip, and I knew if Dad could hit him there, it would look like the deer slowed down enough, thus not having the television station pull the show for breaking their "no running" rule.

It worked. At the instant I said, "Take him!" Dad pulled the trigger on the running buck. I've seen Dad shoot many animals over the years, several of which were running. He's one of the best rifle shots I've ever seen.

As soon as the buck lunged up out of the little dip, you could see him wince from the bullet's impact. The camera man nailed the footage, and when we talked about how we "let the buck slow for the shot," that was all the channel needed to justify airing the program. To tell you the truth, even upon close inspection of the film, it was hard telling how fast that buck was actually moving.

It's funny, because virtually every blacktail hunter I know who watched that episode commented on Dad's classic blacktail shot. It was off-hand, through brush at a buck on a dead-out run. And he made a perfect hit, a one shot kill that dropped the buck on film.

The gun Dad made the shot with was even more impressive, a Thompson Center Pro Hunter chambered in .300 Winchester magnum. The caliber

This was perhaps the most memorable hunt Dad and I ever shared together.
The fact Dad made an incredible, 200 yard running shot on the buck,
all under the pressures of TV and on a land that carried a $12 million price tag,
greatly added to the exuberance of it all.

and make weren't the impressive part; the impressive part was that it was a single-shot rifle.

Dad knew there was a lot on the line. He knew about the "no running shot" rule, that he'd only get one crack at this buck, and that if he missed, there would be no episode to showcase this 12 million dollar piece of real estate.

The buck was running away and slightly at an angle, meaning Dad had to take a slight lead on the buck. With the big objective lens of the 2.5-10x56 Trijicon scope, it was easy for Dad to find and track the buck as it ran.

The bullet entered behind the last rib, slicing through the liver and entering into the lungs. The shot distance, 201 yards. The buck carried nearly 150-inches of antler, one of the largest blacktails Dad had ever taken, and by far the most valuable in terms of coming away with a TV show. That's why we affectionately refer to him as the $12 million blacktail.

Chapter 25:

Muy Grande Or Bust!

Sonora is renowned for holding big mule deer, and on these hunts, I had my sights set on big bucks. One buck was so big, he became a two year obsession.

Sonora, Mexico is one of those magical mule deer places that we all hear about and dream of one day hunting. Growing up I read every story I could on the monster muleys this place produced, but knew I'd likely never be able to afford such a hunt. Then outdoor television came along, and that all changed.

Believe me, I know how fortunate I am to be working in the world of outdoor television, for without it, I would not be experiencing so many hunts I only thought would be dreams. That's why I feel so compelled to share these hunts through the written word, to let more people feel what it's like hunting these magical lands we all desire, but may not get to.

On my first hunt with good friend and outfitter, Jeremy Toman, we were on one of his leased ranches near Hermosillo. It was mid-January, 2007, and the mule deer rut was on. However, severely cold weather made the conditions nearly intolerable for the thin-skinned deer in the area. Due to the biting cold, deer were bedding tight in the brush, and not moving much at all. Some of the locals said it was the worst cold-snap they'd ever seen. This didn't keep us from hunting, though we didn't see near the number of bucks Jeremy was used to.

One of the first bucks we spotted was nearly a mile away. Through the binoculars it was easy to see he was a nice deer, even at that distance. "He's pushing 29-inches wide," shared Jeremy. "I can't tell how his splits are, but his mass is exceptional," he mumbled, now looking through the spotting scope. "Let's go get a closer look."

Fifteen minutes later we were within 300 yards of the buck. He was bedded atop a slight knoll, his harem of does surrounding him. As the glaring sun edged higher into the crisp, morning sky, the buck grew warm. He stood, stretched, then laid down again, giving us a great look at every side of his rack.

"He's a nice buck," Jeremy smiled. "But he's only about 180-inches, maybe 182. I think we can do better."

With that, Jeremy folded up the legs of the tripod, shoved the spotting scope in his pack, and soon we were looking for another deer. I had to remind myself we were in Sonora, where 180-inch bucks can be passed.

Each day we saw bucks, nice bucks. But you could tell Jeremy wasn't happy. "We should be seeing 50 to 70 deer a day on this property, and three times the big bucks we're spotting," he grimaced.

No doubt the severe cold snap had slowed the rut – or at least deer movement. For nearly a week straight, nighttime temperatures plummeted into the low 20s. A few of those days only saw the mercury rise to 38 degrees as a high. Combine this with high winds, and it's no wonder these lean deer, who have no use for storing body fat for the winter, were holed-up in thick brush.

Still, we kept after it, but you could tell the cold was taking it's toll on the deer. What early morning bucks we did see were not chasing does, rather standing in the sun, obviously struggling to maintain body heat.

The good thing, because it took so long to warm up, deer were active all day, which meant some of the best hunting came at midday, when the sun was at its zenith. Over the course of the next few days, we'd see many good bucks in the 165 to 175-inch class, and another pushing 180-inches, but I didn't pull the trigger.

Finally, on the second to the last day of the hunt, a weather change eased in. That night, for the first time since I'd arrived in camp, it didn't freeze. The next morning, bucks were on the move, and without so much as a word, spirits lifted. A nice 4x4 was spotted just outside of camp, but we let him walk.

Soon we came across another buck, and his high, heavy frame caught our attention. He ran across the road in front of us, then stood in a small clearing. Before we could get another look at him, he was off. Though our glimpse was only brief, we could tell the buck seemed nervous, not from our presence, but from something else.

Hiking toward where we last saw him, the answer soon revealed itself. Cracking brush and the sound of clashing antlers left no question the buck was in a fight. Trying to gain a vantage point, all we could see was the tops of swaying branches where the fight was taking place. Capitalizing on the chaotic moment, we wasted no time edging closer.

170

Now within 175 yards of the bucks, all we needed was a break. "Get ready, they quit fighting, maybe he'll step out," whispered Jeremy. "Here he comes!" Just as I clicked off the safety, Jeremy nudged my shoulder. "Wait, there's a bigger buck," he quietly urged.

A closer look at the second buck did prove him to be wider than the first, pushing the prized 30-inch mark, in fact. But an even closer look through the binoculars showed that he'd broken four of his, what should have been, 10 points.

"The first buck is still a nice one, go ahead and take it if you like him," Jeremy anxiously piped. That was all I needed to hear. As my buck tried separating himself from the broken-tined brute, I followed him in the scope. Just as I took the shot, the broken-tine buck moved toward my deer, ready for another battle. Fortunately, the Nosler bullet was already on the way, and the buck didn't go more than 20 yards after the hit.

While he wasn't the biggest buck we saw on this, my first hunt to Sonora, given the conditions he wasn't one I was going to pass up.

He wasn't the biggest buck, carrying just shy of 180-inches of antler, but time was running out. We'd gone down to film a TV show with Jeremy, and with a high-end hunt like this on the line, I had no intentions of going home empty handed.

That afternoon it started to warm up, and on the last day, it got downright hot, like it was supposed to be in Sonora that time of year. With the weather change came increased buck activity. Though my tag was filled, I couldn't help but go out that final day, just to see if there was an increase in deer movement.

Thirty minutes from camp we came across the biggest buck of the entire trip. He was bedded 70 yards from us. His exceptionally massive, high, 6x6 rack spanned close to 30-inches with the five-inch kicker that went out to the side. He would have carried an easy 190-inches of antler, maybe more. All we could do was watch him.

In the next valley, one we'd driven through every day of our hunt and only sporadically seen deer, there were 16 bucks in view, two of which were over 180-inches. That evening, a 31-inch wide 4x5 would stare at us from barely over 100 yards away. In awe, I just watched these mammoth bucks.

Usually I try to hold out for an exceptional animal on every hunt. This time I didn't, and it cost me. I got caught up in the moment of being in Sonora and wanting to fulfill the obligations of getting a TV show, and I missed getting the biggest buck of the trip due to my decision. But, we did come away with a solid TV show, achieving one important objective.

The good part, that final day marked the last day of the season for Jeremy, and he invited me back to hunt the following year. Late in December of 2008, I got a call from Jeremy, "They just saw your buck," was all he said. That was all he had to say. I knew "they" meant the trackers, and I knew what buck they were talking about.

This time I arrived in Sonora the first week of January, hoping to hit the beginning of the rut. The weather was hot and the deer were rutting. To top it off, three days prior to my arrival, the trackers once again spotted my buck. They figured his rack was 32-inches wide, and his forks deeper and heavier than the previous year. "The trackers said he'd go 205 to 207-inches," Jeremy shared. They usually call it within a few inches, so I trusted what was being said.

The first three days of the hunt we spent in the same area where the buck was last seen, very near where we watched him the year prior. Though we didn't see him, I did pass on a 185-inch buck, as well as two others that would have gone 180-inches. That wasn't easy, but I wasn't going to have a repeat of last season's scenario.

On day four of the hunt, we watched a dark-racked brute of a buck chase does across a sparsely vegetated hillside. His rack would have gone 31 to 32-inches wide, but he was only a 3x4. Later that afternoon we passed on another buck, a high, heavy 4x4 that would have pushed 180 inches.

The next morning we gave the area a rest. That's when we received word of a monster buck one of Jeremy's other clients just killed. The hunter was with one of Jeremy's ace guides, and when he said it was a monster buck, my heart sank.

Driving up to the deer, he looked like the one we we'd been after. Then Judas, my local tracker, shook his head. "No, our buck muy grande!" he exclaimed, holding his arms wide and showing the mass with open hands.

Had I seen this buck that lay before us, I would have shot it. He measured 197-inches, and for me, that's muy grande enough. But the tracker insisted it was not the same buck, as was easily evidenced by the lack of that kicker tine on the right side of his rack.

On the second to last day, we saw over 20 bucks, two of which were between 175 and 185-inches. They were rutting hard, fighting, and chasing does.

Using fawn distress calls, we tried pulling does out of the brush, hoping the big buck would follow. Though we called a 170-class buck into range, and other smaller bucks, the big boy didn't show himself.

Don Martin, Jeremy Toman's top guide, led a happy hunter to this 197" Sonora monster muley in the same area I was targeting an even bigger buck.

On the final day of the hunt, first light found us glassing over the area where the buck was last seen. Thick brush and dense cacti made for tedious glassing, but we knew that was the best way to find our buck. That morning we saw some good bucks, but not our buck.

The midday sun was too hot for deer to move, so we went back to camp for a siesta. I couldn't sleep, as I had only one thing on my mind.

For the past year I'd been haunted by this big buck, and now my time was running out. Over the course of the year I'd reviewed the footage of that big buck so many times. On an almost daily basis I would rerun the scene over and over in my mind. I'd wake up many nights, envisioning the buck when I first saw him. He was so regal, so relaxed. He knew we weren't going to shoot him, then. There were many nights I simply could not get back to sleep. Never had I yearned so much for a buck, and never had I been so hard on myself for pulling the trigger on a buck just to get a TV show. Had it not been for the demands of TV, I would have killed this buck on the final morning of that first hunt.

When you attach yourself so closely to a particular animal, it becomes an obsession. The drive for me to complete the job on such animals spawns the ultimate rush, and challenge, which drives me in this business. The thrill of the hunt, and the rewards of catching it on film are of near Super Bowl proportion to me. That's how serious I take this job; that's how rewarding it is to me and how much I love it.

That last afternoon we were back glassing, and I found myself more intently than ever, willing that buck to show up. Then, with only minutes of daylight remaining, a massive bodied buck emerged from a draw and slowly walked up the hillside, away from us.

As Jeremy put the spotting scope on him, I got shooting sticks ready. Through the brush it was hard telling what the buck's rack looked like. Then he stopped.

Cranking my Trijicon 2.5-10x56 scope to full-power, my heart racing, I just knew this was our buck. "All that waiting has paid off," was what I thought to myself as I brought the buck into focus through the scope.

Then, I noticed something was missing. I couldn't see a kicker tine. I looked over at Jeremy to see what he had in the scope, and he just sat there, forehead resting on his spotting scope, staring at the dirt. It wasn't our buck.

With only two minutes of daylight left, we could have shot that buck. He was a dandy, all of 185-inches, but he wasn't the brute we'd set our sights on. Jeremy looked at me, raising his eyebrows in question. "Nope, it's the big one or nothing," I whispered.

As the buck finally walked away, I removed the shells from the rifle. Our hunt was over.

Outfitter, Jeremy Toman, with the results of a fine morning's hunt in Sonora. I've hunted and fished with Jeremy from Alaska to Mexico, and he is among my favorite guys to spend time with. His hard work, fun spirits and knowledge of the animals and the land is something you don't find every day.

"Don't worry, we'll get a TV show," I encouraged Jeremy. We had more big buck footage than any program I'd ever seen, and the fact we got to film that 197-inch buck and another 183-inch buck taken by hunters, helped add to the show. I'm usually against airing TV shows with no kill shots, but this was an exception.

Jeremy invited me back a third year to try for the mysterious, monster buck. Unfortunately, I had a scheduling conflict and couldn't make it. That year, January 2009, the buck moved less than 100 yards off Jeremy's property, and an outfitter on the neighboring lease ended up killing him. It measured 33 1/2-inches wide, was a perfect 6x6 with a seven-inch kicker tine on the right side. He scored 216-inches. Jeremy was too heartsick to even snap a photo of the deer.

That's trophy hunting. Sometimes holding out pays-off, sometimes it doesn't. There are never any guarantees in big game hunting, which makes our sport so appealing. If we knew we were going to fill a tag every time out, what fun would would that be? In hunting, it's the uncertainty that creates the excitement. Besides, if you don't pass on the lesser animals, how will you ever tag a true muy grande?

Conclusion

When I complete a work like this, it's with feelings of ambivalence. I love the gratification that comes with finishing a piece so close to my heart, but at the same time, I'm sad it's over. It's like going on a hunt, really. All the anticipation and excitement building up to those cherished days in the woods, then, when it's all over, the adrenaline let down.

As I neared the completion of this book, reliving these hunts, I found myself getting caught up in them all over again. Typically, my work days would start at 5:00 a.m. and end around midnight. I was nearly as excited to wake up and write these stories as I was to go on the hunts.

I found it difficult to pick and choose the stories to include in these pages, for every hunt holds fond memories I want to share. Of the many books I've penned, it's the adventure titles which lie closest to my heart. The feelings I experienced while writing this book paralleled those felt while writing my first book which detailed my hunting adventures while living in Alaska's arctic. Through the time I took to reflect on the hunts highlighted in this book, I often caught my mind drifting back to those many memories of my Alaskan adventures.

During the years I lived in Alaska's Brooks Range, I was fortunate to take several Dall sheep. This ram, in his long winter fur, was my best one.

My years spent living in Alaska allowed me to partake in some of the most exciting hunts any man could imagine. Without a doubt, these were some of the most cherished hunts I'll ever experience. Living a subsistence lifestyle with the Inupiat Eskimos of Alaska's North Slope region was something very few men in this world have ever experienced, or ever will.

It was here I hunted the towering peaks of the Brooks Range, right out of the village of Anaktuvuk Pass, our home of four years. During that time I took several nice Dall sheep, where, under my sport hunting license and my subsistence permit, I was allowed four sheep a year. It was common to see 150 sheep a day on a single outing. Watching these incredible animals, and having the honor of hunting them in a land where few white men have ever set foot, was a dream come true.

From where I killed my best tundra grizzly, I could look down from the mountains and see our house, tucked near the banks of the Anaktuvuk River. It was common to see caribou every day of the year in this village. One day we counted over 10,000 head of caribou as they walked by my classroom window.

The story behind this tundra grizzly hunt, and all my other Alaskan arctic adventures, were among some of the most memorable of my life. These experiences were detailed in my first ever book, Hunting The Alaskan High Arctic.

Before moving to the Brooks Range, we lived in what's touted as the most remote village in all of Alaska's mainland, Point Lay. From 1990-93, Tiffany and I were two of four school teachers in this village of less than 100 people at the time. Tiffany taught 3rd through 8th grade, every subject; I taught all four grades of high school, every subject. It was hard, but these were some of the most precious years of our lives.

In Point Lay, we lived solely on caribou, along with a smattering of early season waterfowl, ptarmigan and a few fish. During our time in Alaska, the only meat we ate was that which we hunted for. Under my subsistence permit I was allowed five caribou a day, year-round. Needless to say, they made up a large part of our diet.

Growing up in Oregon, I started running my own trap line in fourth grade. I trapped raccoon, beaver, muskrat, red fox and eventually more. I did this so I didn't have to work in the summer, allowing me to fish salmon and steelhead during those months, instead. Learning to trap planted a seed within me, and I yearned to trap in Alaska, as well.

During our years in Alaska, I ran an extensive trap line, where wolf, lynx, wolverine and multiple subspecies of fox were the target. Running a trap line extending more than 100 miles, in temperatures that plummeted to 40 below zero, in total darkness, was a bit different than managing one in Oregon.

Caribou were our primary source of meat for seven years. This bull was my first ever, and my Inupiat Eskimo hunting partner made sure I followed native traditions by having me eat the animal's raw kidney.

While living in Alaska I ran an extensive trap line, taking wolf, wolverine, Arctic fox and lynx. This was my biggest lynx.

One year in Point Lay, we went 199 consecutive days with the temperature holding below zero. Two months of winter were spent in 24 hours of darkness. Arctic storms rushing across the Bering Sea were so intense, drifting snow would literally bury houses. People caught in these storms died, and Tiffany and I almost fell victim to one. In fact, that's the closest I've ever come to death, caught in an Arctic storm.

*During the first year we lived in the tiny Inupiat Eskimo village of Point Lay,
I tracked down and killed this man-eating polar bear. All the blood on the bear is
from the man it killed and ate.*

It was here, in Point Lay, where I tracked down and killed a man-eating polar bear in December of 1990. It was 42° below zero, in total darkness. Pursuing man-eaters adds a whole different dimension to big game hunting.

Why don't I share more of these experiences in this book? Because they've been published in my first book, *Hunting The Alaskan High Arctic*.

What's next? Another hunting book, of course. In fact, I have several titles in the works, with more ideas swimming in my head than I'll ever find time to scribe.

In 1997, when I wrote my first magazine article for Safari Club International's, *Safari* magazine, I knew my life was in for a change. How much of a change, I had no idea, but I did know that my new found passion for writing would lead me down roads I'd only dreamed of one day exploring. I simply chased those dreams and let God lead the way. Today, here I am, working a dream job I thought would forever remain an apparition.

The passions of writing about my hunting experiences and chronicling them on film comes from deep within my heart. For me, this is more than just a hobby. It's a way of life that dominates my every waking moment and fills my thoughts. Hunting is what I love to do and I thank the good Lord for preparing me and giving me the opportunity to live such a blessed life.